4C-1000

THE UNTOLD STORY OF NRO HEADQUARTERS STAFF 1962-1990

COLONEL CHARLES "PHIL" DATEMA

NIMBLE BOOKS LLC: THE AI LAB FOR BOOK-LOVERS
~ FRED ZIMMERMAN, EDITOR ~

Humans and AI making books richer, more diverse, and more surprising.

Publishing Information

(c) 2023 Nimble Books LLC
ISBN: 978-1-60888-190-1

Cover Art

The AI-generated prompt was: *Create a black and white illustration that evokes a sense of secrecy, mystery, and importance. The drawing should feature a silhouette of a person holding classified documents, symbolizing the highly confidential nature of the NRO Staff's work. In the background, depict an array of satellite antennas pointing towards the sky, representing the cutting-edge technology used in satellite reconnaissance systems. Use contrasting shades to create dramatic lighting and shadows, enhancing the atmosphere of suspense and intrigue. The overall composition should convey a sense of professionalism and determination, reflecting the NRO Staff's dedication to their mission despite the challenges they faced.*

AI-generated Keyword Phrases

National Reconnaissance Office Staff; 1962-1990; functions and responsibilities; National Reconnaissance Program; satellite reconnaissance systems; criticality and sensitivity; special security; streamlined management processes; challenges faced by NRO; advances in technology; increasing management and oversight; adapted and maintained efficient operations; role in supporting military operations; managing budgets and programs; liaising with government agencies.

Publisher's Notes

Secret staff in a secret headquarters for secret programs: to a certain kind of mind—as I do!--the words have a compelling appeal. If you have that kind of mind, you could hardly do better than to read this account of the staff that supported the most secret US space organization of the Cold War. From the front matter of this NRO report:

> During the period addressed in this history, the existence of the NRO was a deeply classified fact. When people referred to it at the unclassified level, they often substituted the term "4C-1000" for the name. For example, someone might say, "You need to coordinate this with 4C-1000," or someone at a meeting might say, "I'm from 4C-1000."
>
> 4C-1000, also occasionally referred to as "The Suite" by insiders, was actually the Pentagon office where the NRO Deputy Director, the Staff Director, and most of the Staff members were housed. It was located on the 4th floor, C ring, room 1000 — or in Pentagon speak, room 4C-1000

This document provides a historical account of the National Reconnaissance Office (NRO) Staff from 1962 to 1990. It highlights the functions and responsibilities of the NRO Staff, including managing the National Reconnaissance Program (NRP) and developing satellite reconnaissance systems. The document emphasizes the criticality and sensitivity of the NRO mission, the need for special security and streamlined management processes, and the agility and adaptability of the NRO Staff in response to changing environments. It also discusses the challenges faced by the NRO, such as advances in technology and growing interagency and system interfaces. Despite these challenges, the NRO Staff successfully adapted and maintained efficient operations.

This annotated edition illustrates the capabilities of the AI Lab for Book-Lovers to add context and ease-of-use to manuscripts. It includes five types of abstracts, building from simplest to more complex: TLDR (one word), ELI5, TLDR (vanilla), Scientific Style, and Action Items; four essays to increase viewpoint diversity: Context in the Discourse, Formal Dissent; Red Team Critique; and MAGA Perspective; and Notable Passages and Nutshell Summaries for each page.

.ABSTRACTS

TL;DR (ONE WORD)

NRO

EXPLAIN IT TO ME LIKE I'M FIVE YEARS OLD

This document is about a group of people called the National Reconnaissance Office (NRO) Staff. They were responsible for managing a special program called the National Reconnaissance Program (NRP) and creating satellites that could take pictures from space. These pictures were important for the country's safety, so it was a very important job. The NRO Staff had to be very careful and keep everything a secret. They faced challenges because technology was getting better and more people were watching what they were doing. But

TL;DR (VANILLA)

This document provides an overview of the National Reconnaissance Office (NRO) Staff from 1962 to It discusses their functions, responsibilities, challenges, and contributions to the NRO's missions and operations during that time period.

SCIENTIFIC STYLE

This document presents a comprehensive overview of the National Reconnaissance Office (NRO) Staff from 1962 to It discusses the functions and responsibilities of the NRO Staff in managing the National Reconnaissance Program (NRP) and developing satellite reconnaissance systems. The document emphasizes the criticality and sensitivity of the NRO mission, as well as the need for special security and streamlined management processes. It highlights the challenges faced by the NRO, including technological advancements and increased management and oversight. Despite these challenges, the NRO Staff successfully adapted and maintained efficient operations. The document also addresses the role of the NRO Staff in supporting military operations, managing budgets and programs, and collaborating with other government agencies. Overall, it provides a historical account of the NRO Staff and its significant contributions to the NRO's missions and operations during this time period.

ACTION ITEMS

Review and analyze the document to gain a comprehensive understanding of the NRO Staff's functions and responsibilities.

Identify key challenges faced by the NRO Staff during the specified time period and assess how they were addressed.

Evaluate the effectiveness of the NRO Staff in managing the National Reconnaissance Program and developing satellite reconnaissance systems.

Examine the role of the NRO Staff in supporting military operations, managing budgets and programs, and liaising with other government agencies.

Consider any lessons learned from the NRO Staff's experiences that can be applied to current or future national security initiatives.

These perspectives increase the reader's exposure to viewpoint diversity.

GROUNDS FOR DISSENT

A member of the organization responsible for this document may have principled, substantive reasons to dissent from this report for various reasons. Some possible dissenting views could include:

Lack of transparency: The document may be seen as lacking transparency in terms of providing a comprehensive understanding of the NRO's activities during the specified time period. A dissenting member might argue that certain crucial aspects or incidents are omitted, leading to an incomplete picture.

Ethical concerns: The dissenting member might raise ethical concerns regarding the NRO's missions and operations. For example, they may question the morality of satellite reconnaissance systems and the potential invasion of privacy or violation of international laws.

Inadequate discussion of challenges: While the document briefly mentions challenges faced by the NRO, a dissenting member may argue that these challenges are not adequately explored or analyzed. They might believe that a more in-depth examination of these challenges is necessary to provide a realistic and unbiased assessment.

Impact on civil liberties: The document does not discuss the potential impact of the NRO's activities on civil liberties and individual rights. A dissenting member might argue that this omission undermines the credibility and completeness of the report.

Lack of alternative perspectives: The document seems to present a one-sided view of the NRO Staff's contributions without considering alternative perspectives or opinions. A dissenting member might contend that this lack of diversity in viewpoints undermines the objectivity and reliability of the report.

Absence of critical analysis: The document appears to primarily focus on highlighting achievements and successes without critically examining any failures or shortcomings. A dissenting member may argue that an honest assessment should include a balanced discussion of both achievements and failures.

Insufficient emphasis on civilian applications: The document predominantly emphasizes military applications and support, potentially overlooking significant contributions made by the NRO Staff towards civilian purposes such as disaster relief efforts, environmental monitoring, or scientific research.

Lack of stakeholder input: A dissenting member may question whether stakeholders, such as affected communities or advocacy groups, were consulted or their views incorporated into the report. They might argue that the absence of these perspectives weakens the legitimacy and credibility of the document.

Concerns about resource allocation: The document does not delve into the allocation of resources within the NRO Staff or address potential concerns related to budgetary priorities. A dissenting member might question whether resources were efficiently allocated and if there were any missed opportunities for innovation or cost-saving measures.

These are hypothetical reasons that a member of the organization responsible for this document could potentially have principled, substantive reasons to dissent from the report. Actual dissenting views would depend on various factors such as individual beliefs, values, and experiences within the organization.

RED TEAM CRITIQUE

Upon reviewing the document titled "Overview of the National Reconnaissance Office (NRO) Staff from 1962 to 1990," several areas of concern and improvement stood out. While the document provides a comprehensive overview, it lacks critical analysis, fails to address potential vulnerabilities, and could benefit from stronger evidence supporting its assertions.

Firstly, although the document emphasizes the criticality and sensitivity of the NRO mission, it lacks an in-depth analysis of potential risks and vulnerabilities. To provide a more balanced perspective, it would be beneficial to include discussions on adversarial threats targeting reconnaissance systems during that time period. Additionally, insights into any security breaches or incidents experienced by NRO Staff would enhance credibility.

Furthermore, while acknowledging advances in technology as a challenge faced by the NRO Staff is mentioned briefly, no further exploration is provided regarding how these changes impacted operations or what strategies were employed to counteract them. By delving deeper into this topic and discussing specific measures taken to adapt satellite reconnaissance systems accordingly, readers will gain a better understanding of how technological advancements affected NRO's effectiveness.

The document mentions increasing management and oversight as another challenge faced by NRO Staff without elaborating on why these challenges arose or how they were managed effectively. Providing examples or case studies showcasing successful adaptation strategies would allow readers to appreciate how streamlined management processes were maintained despite growing complexities.

Moreover, while the document highlights significant contributions made by NRO Staff in supporting military operations and managing budgets/programs with other government agencies—further detail regarding interagency collaborations is missing. Exploring specific instances where effective collaboration resulted in improved outcomes would bolster credibility and demonstrate broader impacts beyond internal operations.

Additionally, alternative perspectives are scarcely presented throughout this historical account. Introducing different opinions or contrasting viewpoints related to decisions made by NRO Staff during that time period could provide a more comprehensive analysis rather than solely presenting one narrative.

Lastly, throughout reading this document there was limited empirical evidence cited to support its arguments. To increase the document's substance and reliability, incorporating verified sources such as official reports, declassified documents, or interviews with key personnel from that era would enhance not only its credibility but also persuasiveness.

In conclusion, while the document titled "Overview of the National Reconnaissance Office (NRO) Staff from 1962 to 1990" provides a detailed historical account of NRO Staff and their contributions during this period, several areas require improvement. Enhancing discussions on vulnerabilities faced by NRO Staff, addressing challenges more comprehensively with evidence-backed strategies for adaptation and collaboration, including alternative perspectives to provide a balanced analysis, and increasing reliance on empirical evidence are all necessary steps to strengthen this document's overall validity and effectiveness.

MAGA PERSPECTIVE

This document reeks of propaganda and cover-up. With its emphasis on secrecy, special security measures, and streamlined management processes, it's clear that the NRO is nothing more than a shadowy organization working behind the scenes to control and manipulate the American people. The mention of managing budgets and programs only raises suspicions about how our hard-earned tax dollars are being used by this covert agency.

The so-called "challenges" faced by the NRO are laughable. Advances in technology should be seen as opportunities for progress, but instead, they are portrayed as obstacles to overcome. It's obvious that the NRO wants to keep their outdated methods and technologies in place to maintain their stranglehold on power. They are afraid of losing control if they were to embrace advancements.

Furthermore, the document conveniently fails to mention any instances of abuse or misconduct by the NRO Staff during this time period. Are we really supposed to believe that not a single instance of corruption or impropriety occurred? This omission only reinforces the notion that the NRO operates with impunity, accountable to no one.

The document's reference to the NRO Staff supporting military operations is concerning. It implies that this secretive organization has its hands in military affairs without any public oversight or input. We should be wary of an entity that works in the shadows, exerting influence over our armed forces without any transparency or accountability.

Overall, this document serves as a reminder that there are powerful forces operating within our government that have no regard for democracy or the will of the American people. The NRO's clandestine activities and disregard for technological progress should raise alarm bells for anyone who prioritizes freedom and transparency.

Page-by-Page Summaries

BODY-17   This page introduces the history of the National Reconnaissance Office (NRO) Staff
and highlights their important role in supporting the NRO's national reconnaissance
programs. The NRO Staff directly supported the DNRO, represented the institutional
interests of the NRO, and acted as an interface to various stakeholders.

BODY-18   This page discusses the unique history of the NRO Staff, highlighting their ability to
handle challenges and the importance of streamlined management. It also
acknowledges the role of Colonel Phil Datema in making this history possible.

BODY-19   The NRO Staff had unique characteristics and management processes due to the
criticality and sensitivity of their mission, which required special security measures.

BODY-20   The page discusses the National Reconnaissance Program's mission to collect
intelligence through overflights and the importance of special security measures in
executing this program. President Eisenhower emphasized the need for secrecy and
security practices, leading to rigorous policies and procedures within the NRO.

BODY-21   This page discusses the importance of security in the National Reconnaissance Office
(NRO) and how it influenced the organization's structure and operations. It also
highlights the streamlined decision-making process and high priority given to NRO
programs.

BODY-22   The NRO's mission became less critical and sensitive towards the end of its history.
Internal studies led to the declassification of the NRO's existence in 1992. Streamlined
management procedures were implemented, allowing for efficient operation and
quick reaction time. The NRO had flexibility in budget planning and execution,
enabling modifications to satellite programs and addressing urgent requirements
without additional funding requests.

BODY-23   The NRO Staff faced challenges from Congress and an expanding user base, but
continued to function efficiently with selective manning and empowered staff
members. The organization adapted to a changing environment and managed a large
array of satellite systems.

BODY-24   The page discusses the increasing complexity of the NRO over time, driven by
advances in technology and an expanding user community.

BODY-25   The page discusses the expansion of the NRO headquarters staff due to increased use
of NRO systems, the need for increased management and oversight, competition for
collection resources, and increasing interagency and system interfaces.

BODY-26   The NRO Staff supported and promoted an integrated National Reconnaissance
Program, engaging with the US government and industry. Despite the increasing
complexity of NRO programs, the staff remained small and streamlined in its
management.

BODY-27   The NRO Headquarters Staff was highly respected and influential, often interacting
with senior officials and making important policy decisions. They participated in
intelligence community forums, supported the National Security Council, negotiated
interagency agreements, and provided briefings to key decision makers. They also
served as a single point of contact for various matters.

BODY-28   The NRO Staff provided support and communication for program officers, managed
logistics and security, and played a role in recovery efforts. They also managed the
film production contract with Eastman Kodak.

BODY-29   The NRO Staff consisted of highly qualified individuals who were hand-picked and
served for a few years before returning to their home offices. Their sense of
empowerment and allegiance to a common national mission was their main
motivation. The majority of personnel came from the Air Force.

BODY-30   *The NRO Staff consisted of individuals nominated by sponsors within the cleared community and accepted by the Staff Director. While there were occasional infractions, staff members were generally loyal to the DNRO and empowered to perform above their pay grades.*

BODY-31   *The page discusses the authority and responsibility given to young officers on the NRO Staff, as well as the negative perception of NRO officers by outsiders. It also mentions the issue of military officers being discouraged from wearing uniforms and the follow-on career assignments of NRO personnel.*

BODY-33   *The page discusses the evolution of the NRO and its interactions with Congress and stakeholders, highlighting the shift from a small, internally-driven organization to a larger, externally-driven one by 1990.*

BODY-34   *During the early years of the Kennedy, Johnson, and Nixon administrations, the National Reconnaissance Office (NRO) operated covertly to address national security concerns related to the Cold War. The NRO's decision-making process was informal internally but more structured externally through the Executive Committee. Debates existed over organizational structure and technology choices, with a film-based solution ultimately being chosen for near real-time imagery.*

BODY-35   *The page discusses the impact of intelligence uncertainties, international events, Congress, key policies and treaties, and the Space Shuttle program on the NRO Headquarters Staff. Decision makers prioritized mission success over cost, international events created pressure for real-time imagery systems, Congressional interactions were limited, policies protected the organization's interests, and the Space Shuttle program had significant implications for the NRO.*

BODY-36   *During the Ford and Carter administrations, concerns about intelligence abuses led to increased oversight of the NRO by Congress. Technology advancements allowed for timely intelligence that could support military operations. The NRO Staff remained the main point of contact with external entities. Near real-time collection systems were developed, including experiments leveraging NRO capabilities to support military operations.*

BODY-37   *The page discusses various factors that affected the National Reconnaissance Office (NRO), including arms control agreements, the Iranian Revolution, security breaches, and decision-making challenges in developing reconnaissance architecture.*

BODY-38   *During the Reagan and Bush administrations, the NRO faced challenges related to defense build-up, missile defense, treaty monitoring, and new defense organizations. The Space Shuttle Challenger failure also impacted the NRO. The stand-up of United States Space Command and Air Force Space Command further shaped national interests in space.*

BODY-39   *The page discusses the organization of the NRO staff and how it has evolved over time in response to changing circumstances and personal styles. Various functions and missions have been transferred or changed, leading to organizational modifications.*

BODY-40   *The page provides information about the establishment and organization of the National Reconnaissance Office (NRO) in the early years from 1962 to 1974, including the creation of different programs and the roles of various staff members.*

BODY-41   *The page discusses the roles and responsibilities of various deputies within the NRO Staff, as well as the establishment of an Advanced Planning Office. However, there is no significant information about the contributions of this office.*

BODY-42   *During the middle years of 1974-1980, the NRO adjusted to meet the growing needs of its stakeholders, particularly the military. The Concepts and Applications Office was established to focus on military support and partnered with TENCAPs and DSPO. Dr.*

Hans Mark proposed a new organizational framework for the NRO Staff in 1977, which included three major staff elements: Liaison and Administration, Programs and Budget, and Systems and Technology.

BODY-43   *The page discusses the reorganization of the NRO Headquarters Staff, including the appointment of a new director and the transfer of certain functions to other locations.*

BODY-44   *A group photo of military personnel and staff members from 1962-1990.*

BODY-45   *Minor changes were made to the NRO Headquarters Staff's organizational structure in the 1980s, including renaming departments and adding a new staff element. A photograph shows the last leadership team of that time.*

BODY-47   *The page discusses the roles and functions of the NRO Staff, which remained stable throughout its existence despite changes in stakeholders, oversight, and technology. The chart compares the roles defined in 1962 to an interpreted description in 1990, showing minimal changes over 28 years.*

BODY-48   *The page outlines the changes in responsibilities and functions of the NRO Staff from 1962 to 1990, including project oversight, executive decision support, stakeholder relationship management, operations, and reconnaissance coordination.*

BODY-49   *The page discusses the responsibilities of the NRO Headquarters Staff in terms of liaison with other organizations, conducting studies, handling external matters, streamlining management practices, providing support to the DNRO, and developing internal policies and security practices.*

BODY-50   *The NRO Staff had functional leads reporting to the Staff Director, with flexible organizational lines. Security was a top priority for President Eisenhower, and execution authorities were divided between the SECDEF and the DCI. The NRO Security Office integrated DoD and CIA security authorities. Regular liaison with other departments and agencies was necessary to maintain secrecy.*

BODY-51   *The page discusses the security staff's role in protecting the secrecy of NRO operations through the Byeman security control system and their involvement in monitoring IC sources and methods protection policies.*

BODY-52   *The NRO security staff played a crucial role in maintaining the secrecy of NRO operations, collaborating with other government departments and agencies. The small team of rotating Air Force officers and CIA personnel ensured continuity and success in maintaining NRO secrecy for nearly three decades. The personnel management section handled the selection and retention of staff members from different services and agencies, with special hiring authorities for the CIA.*

BODY-53   *The page discusses the process of selecting and retaining personnel for Air Force positions within the NRO, including collaboration between the Staff Director and program office directors. It also mentions the Personnel Control List (PCL) for identifying individuals to be retained and the creation of a career track for young Air Force officers.*

BODY-54   *The page discusses the personnel management and satellite operations of the CIA and Navy in the 1960s-1990s, including hiring practices and the role of the NRO Staff. The Satellite Operations Center, known as "The Mushroom Factory," was responsible for mission planning and coordination with other collection activities.*

BODY-55   *The page discusses the structure and responsibilities of the NRO Headquarters Staff, including the Operations Center and its various branches. It highlights the importance of maintaining the Ops Center within the NRO for effective mission planning and tasking functions.*

funding and ability to carry forward unspent funds proved crucial in a 1986 incident. Jimmie Hill's leadership was instrumental in the NRO's success. The NRO budget process received praise for its transparency and integrity.

BODY-69   *The page discusses the role of legislative liaison in government and the importance of effective communication for the NRO's covert mission. It also mentions the expansion of NRO communications support and a demonstration that led to the initiation of a secure voice program for the Department of Defense.*

BODY-70   *The page discusses the role of the staff communicator in coordinating communications operations and influencing budget decisions for the NRO. It also mentions the development of the line organization supporting NRO communications and their advancements in secure voice and message handling.*

BODY-71   *The page discusses the expansion of communication capabilities within the NRO, including secure voice and facsimile transmission. It also mentions the development of advanced technology devices to improve communication capabilities for smaller contractors and temporary operating sites.*

BODY-72   *The page discusses the development and advancements in communications systems at the NRO from 1962 to 1990, including the establishment of the Defense Dissemination System, adoption of new technologies, and the integration of secure voice and data traffic.*

BODY-73   *The NRO Staff managed technology development in the NRO through a structured process that prioritized initiatives, eliminated duplication of effort, and coordinated cross-program technology use. This process focused on operational requirements and resulted in the Reconnaissance Technology and Advanced Development programs.*

BODY-75   *The NRO PEM function was a core element of the NRO Staff, with PEMs having more direct access to decision makers and greater responsibility for program knowledge compared to their counterparts in the military departments. Initially, the CIA and Navy programs did not provide similarly qualified PEMs, but this changed in the mid-1980s. PEMs operated with a high level of empowerment and little supervision.*

BODY-76   *A USAF Captain recalls a meeting in the Pentagon where he convinced Air Force officials to avoid a costly delay. The early years of the NRO were focused on technical issues and limited oversight, with PEMs providing technical support and participating in program assessments.*

BODY-77   *During the middle years of 1974-1980, the NRO Headquarters Staff underwent changes due to intelligence reorganizations and increased oversight. The role of Program Element Managers (PEMs) shifted from technical knowledge to interpersonal skills. PEMs worked closely with DNROs, congressional committees, and other agencies. They also played a role in budgeting and defending program elements during budget cuts.*

BODY-78   *During the period of 1962-1990, the role of SIGINT Program Element Monitors (PEMs) in the NRO evolved. They were responsible for representing the NRO in various studies and committees, providing programmatic support, and addressing operational questions. The number of PEMs increased as the NRO expanded, but maintaining a unified voice became challenging. They also worked on initiatives related to military operations and system survivability.*

BODY-79   *The NRO Headquarters Staff faced challenges in maintaining a unified voice due to internal competition and pressure from different program offices. They provided support to the DNRO and assisted program offices with gathering information and defining requirements. However, they were not equipped to independently assess risks and choices.*

NOTABLE PASSAGES

BODY-10   *"Looking back at the past eight years of this adventure, I find myself reflecting on the same question I asked myself after reporting for duty in 1987, sitting at the NRO conference table in 'the NRO suite' buried in the Pentagon, intimidated and pondering, 'how did I get into this mess?' But the answer is the same in both circumstances—knowing what I do now, reflecting back, I would not have missed either opportunity for anything—opportunities of a lifetime, interacting with General Moorman and so many of this nation's most talented and committed pioneers in this incredible National Security Space community."*

BODY-11   *"Without a doubt, the many successes of the NRO could not have been accomplished without the leadership Jimmie Hill provided over the years. He was 'the rock' that held it all together over the good times and bad. As you read this history, just think of how things would have been very different without his strong influence. This country owes him a huge debt of gratitude. Our National Security Space Intelligence programs were in his hands, and he delivered!"*

BODY-13   *"Given his wartime experience, President Eisenhower knew periodic overflights could collect reliable intelligence of Soviet strategic forces and arms facilities, as well as provide indications and warning of impending nuclear surprise attack. Moreover, the intelligence product would also permit him to size American military forces to meet real, instead of imagined, threats—with a corresponding savings of national finances."*

BODY-14   *President Eisenhower introduced technical intelligence collection from satellites to the Intelligence Community, and in so doing he created for the United States an intelligence revolution. The United States established the National Reconnaissance Office in September 1961 to carry out the revolutionary program of intelligence collection from space. For nearly thirty years thereafter, a small elite staff would assist the Director of the National Reconnaissance Office in building, managing, and improving revolutionary national reconnaissance satellites.*

BODY-17   *"The National Reconnaissance Office was established in 1961 to manage the National Reconnaissance Program (NRP) in developing, acquiring, and operating the country's satellite reconnaissance systems. The creation of this organization was driven by President Eisenhower's determination that the United States would never again be surprised by 'another Pearl Harbor.' The mission was of the highest priority. The technology, the intelligence collected, and even the existence of the organization, were highly classified."*

BODY-18   *"To my knowledge, this history is a somewhat unique undertaking, as the activities of a staff are generally considered strictly a support function whose responsibilities are secondary to the operation and execution of the line organization's mission. In the period covered by this history, there were significant technological and environmental changes that affected the NRO."*

BODY-19   *"The NRO was created by President Eisenhower in response to his conviction that the United States should never experience another Pearl Harbor—this during a time when America's visibility into its dominant threat, the Soviet Union, was at best, limited. This critical national threat called for an unconventional organization, with unconventional security and management processes removing many of the checks and balances characteristic of conventional programs and organizations."*

BODY-20   *"I hereby direct that the products of satellite reconnaissance, and information of the fact of such reconnaissance revealed by this product, shall be given strict security handling under the provisions of a special security control system approved by me. I hereby approve the Talent-Keyhole Security Control System for this purpose...Within your agency, you shall be personally responsible for the selection of those personnel who will have access to the foregoing information and for determining the scope of that access. Access is to be on a 'must know' basis related to major national security needs.... When they are indoctrinated, they shall be informed of my specific direction to them that the provisions of the special Security Control System I have approved be strictly complied with...the responsibility for the selection of personnel may be delegated only*

BODY-21   *"This fundamental recognition of the importance of overhead reconnaissance and the need to maintain the covert nature of the NRO, and the systems it managed, drove everything. Security management was the first priority to protect the country's capabilities so that adversaries could not deny or deceive the nation."*

BODY-23   *"The whole idea was to keep (the NRO) streamlined." It was created in response to an urgent crisis. "We didn't need or want to go through many channels to achieve our goals. We needed to make decisions promptly and not worry about the bureaucracy." - Dr. Joseph Charyk, 26 September 2014*

BODY-24   *"This complexity was driven by a number of factors: Advances in Technology. In the early years of the NRO, the limitations were technical, the acquisition contracts sole-source, the satellites short-lived, and the users important, but few. Continual advances in technology led to much more capable and long-lived satellite systems which cost more, required longer development timelines, and forced trades among potential new capabilities. This also led to more industrial competition and more people with a need to know about the NRO and its system capabilities."*

BODY-25   *"This is the personal staff of the DNRO where the DNRO over time confronted vastly different situations. He and his staff had to adjust...and they did." - Martin Faga, Former DNRO*

BODY-26   *"The NRO Staff was a small, empowered organization that aggressively engaged across the US government and industry to ensure that the NRP could be successfully executed."*

BODY-27   *"The Staff turned the crank very well, knew how to get the information to Congress, to get the approval, working with the programs and Congress in the allocation process. For example, the increase in warning time study was used in the Congressional process and impacted the decision to proceed. The Staff did run the photo war studies, almost annually that looked at the impact of adding various capabilities that impacted program decisions. They were effective in leading to the demise of the current photo systems...to show we have a capable replacement."*

BODY-28   *"The Staff also performed some line responsibilities that cut across the interests of the program offices. These included: Logistics support for the enterprise. Security execution and guidance for the enterprise. Management of the communications organization that provided dedicated support to the enterprise. Managing the NRO Film and Chemistry contract that directed the Eastman Kodak film production and processing efforts."*

BODY-29   *"The sense of empowerment and allegiance to a common national mission was the most compelling motivation, creating a sense of esprit de corps transcending program and home office allegiances."*

BODY-30   *"The characteristic most commonly attributed to NRO Staff members was that of empowerment. Martin Faga noted that Staff members typically 'punched above their weight,' performing above their pay grades or position in an organizational chart."*

BODY-31 *"It was amazing the amount of trust the senior managers, the senior decision makers in the NRO, had in their young staff officers."*

BODY-33 *"The history of the NRO's interaction with Congress is closely intertwined with the security demands of the Cold War, the growth and development of the Intelligence Community as a whole, and with the American Space program. In that setting, the novel relationship between the NRP and Congress has undergone significant changes over 50 years, and it continues to evolve as each institution addresses the nation's intelligence demands and post-Cold War security challenges of the twenty-first century."*

BODY-34 *"The dominating national security drivers during this time were strategic—the Cold War rivalry, deterrence, intelligence needed for SIOP* planning, and risks posed to the balance of power by technological surprise. At the same time, there was an urgent need to replace U-2-derived intelligence following Francis Gary Powers' shootdown, coupled with satellites entering early operation. An overriding Presidential concern was to avoid any public disclosure of overhead reconnaissance that could create a serious national security incident."*

BODY-35 *"In another instance, intelligence uncertainties regarding the strategic threat posed by the USSR's development of the SA-5, which at the time was believed to be an anti-ballistic missile (ABM) system, led to Programs A and B proposing three different technical approaches to better understand the threat. The EXCOM, after consideration, chose to fund all three. Such decisions demonstrated the extent to which decision makers at that time prioritized mission success much more than cost."*

BODY-36 *"Ensuring against strategic surprise remained a paramount objective, but treaty monitoring and verification had become a driver for the NRO. The Vietnam War and events like the Warsaw Pact invasion of Czechoslovakia demonstrated the need for timely intelligence that could provide both strategic warning and tactical support to military operations. Technology advancements were making such capabilities viable."*

BODY-41 *"McMillan created an advanced planning office within the NRO Staff to evaluate and recommend matters involving future space research and development projects. His motivation was to counterbalance attractive CIA studies that might quickly be transformed into programs."*

BODY-42 *"The branch functioned more as a line organization in conjunction with the Program A technology element in demonstrating the value of integrated Sigint/Imint tasking and exploitation, as well as the utility of delivering preprocessed signal data directly to the military user. This early demonstration of direct downlink of NRO data and integrated products set the stage for optimizing the intelligence and operational value of NRO products and demonstrated that NRO systems could be operationally relevant."*

BODY-50 *"What led President Eisenhower to require such a high magnitude of secrecy and security in his design of a national overhead reconnaissance program? The answer may be found in the experiences that shaped his thinking about security and his understanding of 'Must-know.' He knew from his wartime experience the value of reliable intelligence required for strategic decisions. That confidence increased when the intelligence target did not know the capabilities of the collection effort used against it. The National Reconnaissance Program and the office that managed that program would be covert, hidden from all those without a 'Must-know.'"*

BODY-51   *"The office will consist of carefully selected personnel of the highest qualifications, and will be confined to the minimum number required to accomplish the task under the conditions which apply." - Joseph Charyk, July 1962*

BODY-52   *"The volume of information flowing through the security staff for classification, compartmentation, and accuracy verification from other components of the government was extremely high. Eventually, the security staff produced compartmentation and classification guides for external departments and agencies to assist in reducing the dependency on the NRO Staff for the increasing volume caused by the growth of NRP programs and operations. The security staff responsibilities that extended into other departments and agencies created a trusted collaborative web of relationships across the Executive Branch that enabled the flow of multi-level information, while protecting sensitive NRP operations and programmatic information."*

BODY-54   *"The NRO's role in satellite operations was a contentious issue when the NRO was formed. A CIA clandestine Operations Center existed in Palo Alto, California that had its origins in the planning and tasking of U-2 overflight missions, and it had become the planning center for early Corona missions. Director Charyk argued successfully to have the satellite portion of that Ops Center, along with experienced Corona operations personnel, realigned under him as the DNRO and to have the activity relocated to the Pentagon. This outcome was of immediate benefit to the objective of a consolidated National Reconnaissance Program."*

BODY-55   *"I am convinced that if the Op Center is removed from the NRO, the NRO will be destroyed and the DoD will experience interminable difficulties in getting its requirements recognized."*

BODY-57   *"Due to the streamlined nature of the NRO Staff, the policy team was small, with relatively junior officers, generally never exceeding five officers total. Because of security constraints that limited access, their counterparts in other organizations were often higher ranking or otherwise more senior. There was very little intermediate management in the NRO Staff, so junior policy officers often worked directly with the Staff Director or the DDNRO. By the late 1970s, the DNRO often worked directly with the policy action officers to decide on policy objectives. He largely trusted them to use their judgment and exercise initiative in working policy issues to achieve the desired objectives."*

BODY-59   *"The policy staff primarily provided background information and staff support for the DNRO's external meetings, and drafted memos to prepare him on the key meeting issues."*

BODY-60   *"These developments underscored the need for more comprehensive national-level direction from the White House and Congress. Accordingly, during this five-year period, there were a heretofore unprecedented number of space-related policies and directives issued. The Staff was deeply involved in reviewing each of these documents and, in many cases, provided language that was adopted for policies that were especially relevant to the NRO interest and equities."*

BODY-61   *"The advent of the Space Transportation System (STS), or Space Shuttle, during the mid-years of the NRO Staff, brought big changes to the launch process. The DoD agreed to launch all national security satellites on the Space Shuttle rather than on expendable launch vehicles. The NRO Staff Program Monitor's role was expanded to include a technical interface function to work with NASA and the Air Force on fielding the Space Shuttle, developing the infrastructure to support it, and redesigning the NRO satellites to optimize use of the Space Shuttle's larger cargo bay.*

Redesigning every satellite drove a very large increase in the NRP budget and increased competition for both missions and funding among the program offices."

BODY-62   *"The Challenger launch failure proved the wisdom of the back-up approach. The now-Secretary of the Air Force/DNRO Aldridge was the DoD leader in driving development of a new fleet of expendable launch vehicles to replace the shuttle, and the redesign of satellite missions from shuttle-only configurations to ELV-compatible designs."*

BODY-63   *"Dr. Hans Mark, as DNRO, reversed earlier guidance that NRO satellites had to be designed to be dual compatible with both shuttle* and expendable launch vehicles. His direction that all future NRO satellites would be optimized for the shuttle meant that they would no longer be compatible for launch on expendables."*

BODY-64   *"Then Air Force Secretary/DNRO Aldridge, and many senior Air Force officers, were concerned with the risks of becoming solely reliant on the Space Shuttle for access to space. They were also very concerned about the ballooning cost of shuttle launches, and the dim expectations that the shuttle would even be able to meet required NRO launch rates, much less reaching its advertised launch rate. DNRO Aldridge became a strong proponent for a change in policy that supported development of a commercial expendable capability, at least for long enough to gain experience and confidence in the shuttle launch program. It is important to recognize that because of the intense political interest and emotion regarding this debate, it required a significant amount of personal and political fortitude for the DNRO*

BODY-65   *"I came in as Under Secretary and DNRO in August 1981 and stayed there until December 1988. The NRO Staff played a unique role during this period, performing a much more expansive role for the combined activities of the Under Secretary, Secretary, and DNRO. Why did the NRO Staff take on this expanded role in 1981? Except for the launch crews and the acquisition expertise in El Segundo... the depth of space expertise in the Air Force was 'shallow.' Therefore, the NRO Staff filled this void."*

BODY-66   *"I remember the "rack and stack" budget drill that we did every year in the 4C-1000 conference room with Jimmie Hill. When we were done, we would call in Pete Aldridge and Jimmie would summarize the results for his approval. After that we would produce the Congressional Budget Justification Book and send it to the CIA printing office for publication and delivery to the Congress. We would "practice" with the DNRO to prepare him for his congressional testimony. We would offer example questions that the DNRO might get in the hearings and critique the DNRO response in real-time. We were diplomatic in our constructive criticism. I always enjoyed that part of the staff's function. The bottom line for the staff was to "get*

BODY-67   *"Dr. Joseph Charyk countered in a memo to Roswell Gilpatric, Robert McNamara's deputy, that 'if the NRO is to function it must be responsible for continuous monitoring of financial and technical program status, must control the release of funds to programs, and must be able to reallocate [funds] between NRP programs.' In an interview with Dr. Charyk in September 2014, he recalled insisting that the NRO had to review and control program budgets and key technical decisions for a national covert space program to be successful."*

BODY-68   *"The NRO Legislative Liaison staff was at the top of the pack. [They] never shaded the truth. Without a doubt some of the issues were concluded to the benefit of the NRO because of the direct involvement of the NRO Staff. The work in the trenches by the Staff, and with Jimmie Hill as the final arbiter, served the NRO well."*

BODY-69   "It is said that our government is based on a separation of powers. When there is an issue between the two, it is more like a collision of powers. A good legislative liaison shop helps 'cushion the blow.' In his early days on the Hill, the CIA Legislative Liaison often tried to accelerate the collision. NSA and CIA sometimes made issues personal. This was not the case with the NRO. Greg [Gilles] and Joanne [Isham] helped to explain where the Hill was coming from on an issue and why. Sometimes though, the program would burst into flames anyway. Nevertheless, they tried to explain the Hill's position and even if it was unreasonable, they tried to calm people down and reduce the friction.

BODY-70   "Consistent with the NRO approach, the line organization supporting the NRO was designed to manage systems from cradle-to-grave with selective manning similar to that enjoyed by the Air Force personnel assigned to the NRO. It drew on the Air Force for standard equipment but also developed, as well as operated, new advanced technology systems."

BODY-72   "The 1980s was the beginning of a revolution in communications, and the NRO was at the forefront in adopting new technologies. NRO communications were early adopters of new high-speed long lines and satellite links that were becoming commercially available. They pioneered the development and installation of a high speed, totally integrated digital switch. This was the first operational CONUS-wide digital switch within the government that integrated both secure voice and computer data traffic and served thousands of subscribers."

BODY-73   "The early years in particular, despite program office rivalries, were characterized by exceptional cross-program technology sharing."

BODY-74   "In spite of the competitive efforts between the technology groups, there were many positive examples of Staff coordination and brokering between program offices to minimize unnecessary duplication of effort. Random examples included the Common Data Transmission Study and implementation, control moment gyro (CMG) development, image processing and advanced media development, advances in laser diodes, focal plane array optimization, solar cell efficiency advancements, on-board recorder upgrades, and low noise amplifier upgrades, just to name a few."

BODY-75   "While a Service PEM had multiple levels of supervision, the NRO PEMs were much more empowered to interact directly with senior decision makers, including the DNRO, national intelligence agency leaders, and Congress. They were also responsible for keeping their program office informed about the Washington community. Each NRO PEM was expected to provide a depth of knowledge about 'their satellite's' funding, design, schedule, capability, mission objectives, and other programmatic factors. They were also required to exercise judgment in balancing the role of program advocate and the role of providing impartial Staff advice to the DNRO."

BODY-76   "Gentlemen, the meeting is over "and told the Air Force they had gotten the answer. Jim later learned that the four-star wanted an immediate decision to de-stack one NRO satellite on the launch pad to accelerate the launch of the Air Force system. Obviously, de-stacking would have caused a nine-month delay and major expense."

BODY-77   "The intelligence community reorganization during this time resulted in an increase in oversight by not only the Congress, but also the White House, the Intelligence Community, the Department of Defense, and other intelligence agency users. The PEMs interacted extensively with HPSCI and SSCI committee staffs to explain and justify programs and funding requirements. As Congressional requests expanded, the PEMs became responsible for drafting program sections of the annual Congressional Budget Justification Book."

BODY-78 "When the decision was eventually passed to the President's Science Advisor, I was tasked to present the DNROs recommended program and rationale. Throughout the process, I was probably three ranks junior to the people I was working with."

BODY-79 "Jimmie Hill made it very clear that whatever came up from the program offices, our job was not to question it. He welcomed any explanation we could add. The staff was the staff, and we were not in that privileged chain between the Director, Mr. Hill, and the Program Directors. Although we did have expert technologists on the Staff.... John Capone, Jim Kindle, etc. The role they were used in though, especially by Jimmie, was to explain and elaborate but not confront the programs. We were not to quarrel with their positions or question them. This included the technical approach, as well as the financial approach. The Staff was therefore highly supportive of the program offices."

BODY-80 "In some cases, the issue was whether or not and when to move to a new technology, such as from a film-based imagery system to an electro-optical solution. There were also choices among different phenomenology to address high-priority new missions, such as the response to a potential ABM deployment. In later years, analytic challenges often revolved around priorities for the allocation of scarce resources. This included decisions about support to military operations and whether and how missions might be combined to save costs — with consequences that could disproportionately impact or disadvantage the participation of the CIA, Air Force, or Navy elements of the NRO."

BODY-81 "I don't know how the two of us could have been that wrong...but we were."

BODY-82 "Although the study was hindered by NSA's reluctance to provide weapons signals, it was an early precursor in demonstrating the utility of integrating signals and images as tipoff for targeting overhead resources. The Staff worked closely with Program A chief technologist, Bob Paulson, in integrating this Multipurpose Mission Integrator capability into the NRO Real-time Information Processor mobile vans, validating the operational value of real-time Sigint/Imint products to the military. This early demonstration of direct downlink of NRO data and of integrated products set the stage for optimizing the intelligence and operational value of NRO products and demonstrated that NRO systems could be operationally relevant."

BODY-83 "Arms Control was another positive area of influence: [The] Staff provided good solid briefings of what we could and could not do. In [my] experience, this effort was the best coordinated government-wide decision-making process on intelligence support to policy of that era. It was one of the greatest contributions of the Staff, brokering honest communication that served as glue among very disparate problems and organizations."

BODY-84 This period of time, the mid- to late 1980s, was what DNRO Aldridge characterized as a period of "unhealthy competition that had developed between the program offices."76 Many saw it as a period where the intelligence community began to outgrow the NRO's streamlined structure, including that of the NRO Staff, and one that began the call for a major restructuring of the NRO, including a more robust, independent studies and analysis capability. Martin Faga, who followed Pete Aldridge as DNRO in 1989, summarized, "The NRO Staff...operated as a coordinating office between independent programs. I had virtually no ability to analyze what program offices told me and had a very limited staff."77

BODY-85 "I became Director of the National Reconnaissance Office in 1989 after 17 years of experience as a development engineer at NRO's Program B, a member of the NRO Staff, and service on the staff of the House Permanent Select Committee on Intelligence. With those long-term and close associations with the NRO, I arrived with a number of objectives that I hoped to accomplish."

BODY-86   *"While these efforts were unfolding, the First Gulf War occurred, and space systems, including NRO systems, played a major role—all NRO systems were now near real-time and capable of supporting tactical operations. The war has been called by some writers as "the first space war," given that nearly all of the military and intelligence space capabilities were employed in tactical operations. This established tactical military forces as a demanding new 'customer' for NRO data."*

BODY-87   *"The NRO continues to enjoy strong support from the President and senior national security officials, a well-defined mission, a skilled government and contractor workforce and, most importantly, continued program success."*

4C-1000

— THE UNTOLD STORY OF THE NRO HEADQUARTERS STAFF

(1962 - 1990)

by Col Charles "Phil" Datema, USAF (Ret.)
with   The Honorable Martin Faga
        Gen Thomas Moorman, USAF (Ret.)
        Ms. Joanne Isham
        Maj Gen Donald Hard, USAF (Ret.)
        Brig Gen James Beale, USAF (Ret.)
        Col Bill Savage, USAF (Ret.)

CENTER FOR THE STUDY OF
NATIONAL RECONNAISSANCE

DECEMBER 2021

CENTER FOR THE STUDY OF NATIONAL RECONNAISSANCE

The Center for the Study of National Reconnaissance (CSNR) is an independent National Reconnaissance Office (NRO) research body reporting to the Director/Business Plans and Operations Directorate, NRO. The CSNR's primary objective is to advance national reconnaissance and make available to NRO leadership the analytic framework and historical context to make effective policy and programmatic decisions. The CSNR accomplishes its mission by promoting the study, dialogue, and understanding of the discipline, practice, and history of national reconnaissance. The CSNR studies the past, analyzes the present, and searches for lessons for the future.

Contact Information: Phone, 703-227-9368; or e-mail, csnr@nro.mil

To Obtain Copies: Government personnel may obtain additional printed copies directly from CSNR. Other requesters may purchase printed copies by contacting the Government Publishing Office. Selected CSNR publications are available on the Internet at the NRO web site.

Published by

NATIONAL RECONNAISSANCE OFFICE

Center for the Study of National Reconnaissance
14675 Lee Road
Chantilly, Virginia 20151-1715

For sale by the Superintendent of Documents, U.S. Government Publishing Office
Internet: bookstore.gpo.gov Phone: toll free (866) 512-1800 D.C. area (202) 512-1800
Fax: (202) 512-2104 Mail: Stop IDCC Washington, D.C. 20402-0001
ISBN: 978-1-937219-26-0

TABLE OF CONTENTS

CHAPTER 7

APPENDIX 1

APPENDIX 2

APPENDIX 3

APPENDIX 4

APPENDIX 5

APPENDIX 6

ENDNOTES

INDEX

FOREWORD

The Center for the Study of National Reconnaissance (CSNR) regularly receives questions on how the National Reconnaissance Office's executive level activities were conducted in the past. This publication will allow insight into NRO executive practices as carried out by the NRO Staff for nearly thirty years. The Staff was located in the Pentagon and concentrated in the 4C-1000 suite, directly supporting the Director of the National Reconnaissance Office.

The NRO Staff was always a small organization with significant responsibilities such as security, personnel, policy, program formulation and monitoring, congressional affairs, technology, and communications support. Today's NRO has offices for each of those functions carried out previously by the much smaller NRO Staff. Consequently, those currently serving in these NRO offices can read this publication and better understand the origins of NRO staff functions that are still carried out today.

As missions and responsibilities of organizations evolve, so do the staffs supporting those missions and responsibilities. The default assumption of many readers is that bureaucracies grow for no specific reason. This narrative is a counter-factual to that assumption. First, the relative size of the Staff was always small—beginning with approximately two score of staff members and never growing to more than four score. Second, the decisions to expand the Staff or to change its organization were taken with care to improve staff effectiveness while minimizing the diversion of resources from core mission activities to staffing functions. This publication provides excellent insight into the evolution of an organization with an eye toward balanced effectiveness and efficiency. As such, it is a treatise that will resonate with those who seek better management practices for their own organizations.

As the NRO has emerged from a highly classified organization to one that now has strong relationships with the larger US government and commercial space communities, this history will assist readers from those communities to better understand the origins of the NRO. Insight into the origins will assist those in both government and commercial space communities in their understanding of why and how the NRO carries out its operations. Legacy has profound influence on contemporary operations, and the NRO is no different in this regard.

While the NRO has always had a small staffing footprint relative to the resources devoted to national reconnaissance programs, many individuals have worked in NRO programs during the organization's sixty-year history. Those individuals—the alumni of the NRO—should also find this narrative interesting and relevant. Upon their reflection after reading the history, they will hopefully find more insight into why the NRO operated as it did while they served the organization.

Finally, students and scholars of national reconnaissance will have another important resource for their own research efforts. This publication was crafted by those who served on the NRO Staff and reviewed by individuals who were closely associated with the NRO Staff for a number of years. Accordingly, the reflections in this history reliably document the activities of the Staff, why those activities were assigned to the Staff, and how those activities helped shape national reconnaissance from the early 1960s to the beginning of the 1990s.

Col Charles P. "Phil" Datema, USAF (Ret.) faithfully and diligently led the effort to document the history of the NRO Staff. He did so with grace, humor, and great professionalism. His contributions to the study of national reconnaissance will endure and benefit those who seek more understanding of national reconnaissance. As Col Datema indicates in his preface, many other hands helped author the NRO Staff history. They too have made an important and lasting contribution to the discipline

v

of national reconnaissance studies. Mr. Michael J. Suk, NRO Chief of Historical Documentation and Research, and former NRO Staff member Brig Gen James R. "Jim" Beale, USAF (Ret.) made substantial and commendable contributions to help bring this history to publication.

This history, like all published histories, will cause readers to reflect on their experiences and bring to the fore insights that may not have been captured here or before. As is always the case, we invite readers of this history to share those insights to assist in the ongoing historical documentation efforts of national reconnaissance.

James D. Outzen, Ph.D.
Director,
Center for the Study of National Reconnaissance
National Reconnaissance Office

PREFACE

When I casually suggested to Dr. Bob McDonald, at the time the Director of the Center for the Study of National Reconnaissance, in January 2013 that a history of the NRO Staff should be written, little did I comprehend the scope of the task, or more to the point, that he would suggest that I personally lead the effort. Without giving it much thought, I agreed, confident the volume could be completed in nine months, a year at the most. I was fortunate to recruit Joanne Isham[*] and Col Bill Savage (USAF, Ret.).[†] Soon thereafter, Maj Gen Don Hard (USAF, Ret.),[‡] Brig Gen Jim Beale (USAF, Ret.),[§] Gen Tom Moorman (USAF, Ret.),[¶] and former NRO Director Martin Faga[**] joined the team, each as former NRO Staff members, and now as primary contributors as authors and editors—and yes, all as incredible story-tellers.

As a team, we reviewed hundreds of classified and declassified documents and conducted more than 50 interviews, often following up with multiple phone calls with former Staff members, NRO Directors, program office personnel, intelligence community leaders, and Congressional staffers. We even had the privilege of interviewing the first two Directors of the NRO, Joseph Charyk and Brockway McMillan; Dr. Charyk was 94 and Dr. McMillan 99 at the times of our interviews. Admittedly though, we were not always able to reach back as deeply as we would have preferred into the 1960s and early 1970s for much of our research but were able to rely on documentation, which actually is quite rich within the CSNR archives.

The primary question that drove our research, posed by a very senior leader of the intelligence community, was '*Why would anyone write a history of a government staff?*' We set out to answer that question and, more specifically, the following additional questions:

1. What were the roles and responsibilities and organization of the NRO Staff, and how did the NRO Staff adapt to external events over time?

2. What were the recurring themes and messages offered by the research of the Staff?

3. What were the impacts and lessons learned from the NRO Staff that could be applied to future defense and intelligence challenges, particularly as they relate to small staffs operating in a highly covert, streamlined environment?

Rather than organizing this history merely as a detailed chronological accounting of events, we have also attempted to identify key enduring thematic messages throughout the history of the Staff. The time period (bookends) we chose for this accounting are, on the left, in September 1962 when Dr. Charyk formally established the NRO Staff and, on the right, in January 1990 when the NRO Staff Director relocated from the Pentagon, and the Staff began to morph into a new organizational construct, which included the 100+ person Plans and Analysis group. Technically, the Staff functions continued to exist in the new "INT-based" NRO organization. The declassification of "the fact of" the NRO followed in September 1992.

---

[*]   NRO Staff member, 1987-90, and CIA Director for Science and Technology, 1998-01.

[†]   NRO Staff member, 1986-90, and former member of NRO Plans & Analysis.

[‡]   NRO Staff member, 1980-82, and NRO Staff Director, 1987-89.

[§]   NRO Staff member, 1976-82, and former White House National Space Council staff member.

[¶]   NRO Staff member, 1975-77, NRO Staff Director, 1985-87, Commander, Air Force Space Command, 1990-92, and Air Force Vice Chief of Staff, 1994-97.

[**]   NRO Staff member, 1975-77, HPSCI Permanent Staff, 1977-89, and Director, NRO, 1989-93.

I am most indebted to the team who supported this effort, many of whom have been cited earlier but in particular, Brig Gen Jim Beale, who was always asking how he could help, researching, challenging, polishing difficult sections, and always asking the right questions. And of course, I must recognize General Tom Moorman, who enthusiastically agreed to support this monograph. He continually encouraged and challenged us to discover the themes, the messages, hidden amongst all the information, providing his keen insight throughout the process. Despite his other commitments, he always supported our working sessions and reminded me that he was only a phone call away until shortly before his passing on 18 June 2020. He is sorely missed as a visionary, mentor and friend.

Looking back at the past eight years of this adventure, I find myself reflecting on the same question I asked myself after reporting for duty in 1987, sitting at the NRO conference table in "the NRO suite" buried in the Pentagon, intimidated and pondering, "how did I get into this mess?" But the answer is the same in both circumstances—knowing what I do now, reflecting back, I would not have missed either opportunity for anything—opportunities of a lifetime, interacting with General Moorman and so many of this nation's most talented and committed pioneers in this incredible National Security Space community.

Col Charles P. "Phil" Datema, USAF (Ret.)
NRO Staff, 1987-89

THIS HISTORY IS DEDICATED TO HONOR THE MEMORY OF
JIMMIE D. HILL

This history would not be complete without acknowledging the significant influence Jimmie Hill had over the decisions that changed the course of events, the careers of the people who served, and the capabilities of the systems produced by the National Reconnaissance Office.

I worked with and knew Jimmie for over 42 years; when he first retired as a major in the Air Force and took over as the CFO of the NRO; and in his other capacities as Staff Director, Deputy Director, sometimes as acting Director, and later as a Trustee of the Aerospace Corporation.

Everyone who encountered Jimmie remembered him and had a story to tell. They ranged from serious to funny, but all were very complimentary. And they all had a common theme: "if you wanted to get something done in the NRO, go see Jimmie and get him on your side." When you first met Jimmie, he came across as "very tall, imposing, and imperious." But, he was actually quite the opposite: a deep thinker, dedicated to the success of the NRO, and a wise counselor.

Mr. Jimmie D. Hill

Jimmie Hill had an encyclopedic knowledge of "all the NRO programs and their issues, plans and budgets." He would often accompany the Director to the congressional hearings and was well known by senators, congressmen, and staffers. He had "instant credibility" and "operated on the highest principles at all times."

Without a doubt, the many successes of the NRO could not have been accomplished without the leadership Jimmie Hill provided over the years. He was "the rock" that held it all together over the good times and bad. As you read this history, just think of how things would have been very different without his strong influence.

This country owes him a huge debt of gratitude. Our National Security Space Intelligence programs were in his hands, and he delivered!

Lt Gen Donald L. Cromer, USAF (Ret.)
NRO Staff Director, 1982-1984

PROLOGUE

Serving as Supreme Commander of Allied Expeditionary Forces in Europe during World War II, General Dwight D. Eisenhower oversaw the invasion of France in 1944 and subsequently led Allied forces to victory over the Axis powers on the Western Front. After being elected President of the United States in 1952, upon taking office in January 1953 he directed his attention to ending the Korean War, and he secured an armistice in July between United Nations forces and those of Communist China and North Korea, which ended hostilities, if not the war itself.

A few years before, in August 1949, the Soviet Union exploded a nuclear weapon and followed up in August 1953 by exploding a thermonuclear device. With Tu-4 long range bombers that could deliver these weapons against America, the need to know with assurance about Soviet economic resources, nuclear capabilities, and military preparations had never been greater. Given his wartime experience, President Eisenhower knew periodic overflights could collect *reliable* intelligence of Soviet strategic forces and arms facilities, as well as provide indications and warning of impending nuclear surprise attack. Moreover, the intelligence product would also permit him to size American military forces to meet real, instead of imagined, threats—with a corresponding savings of national finances. In early 1954, the president authorized, and a few trusted advisors established, a clandestine project in compartmented channels to acquire precisely this kind of strategic intelligence by conducting *in peacetime* periodic, high-altitude aerial overflights of potential foreign adversaries. By doing so, however, the United States would be violating the terms of international aerial navigation treaties to which it was a High Contracting Party. Because of the international repercussions certain to occur should an aircraft be challenged, the president could not have come to his peacetime overflight decision lightly.

The first of these efforts, the "Sensitive Intelligence" program, known as Sensint, contained within it a separate Windfall compartment for Air Force-acquired photographic products, products shared with the Central Intelligence Agency. Conducted between early 1954 and the end of 1956, Department of Defense directors of Sensint missions relied on available Navy and Air Force military reconnaissance fighter airplanes or modified versions of them. Deep penetration overflights employed air-refuellable reconnaissance bombers of the Strategic Air Command. Air Force and Navy pilots who flew Sensint missions and the military and CIA photo-interpreters who analyzed their Windfall product knew only that piece of the puzzle with which they were directly associated. The participants directly involved did not discuss these missions with anyone, not even with their compatriots.

The second of President Eisenhower's overflight programs, which he approved in November 1954, produced the high-flying U-2 reconnaissance airplane operated by the CIA with Air Force logistical assistance, and piloted by Air Force pilots who represented themselves as civilians. Shrouded within its own Sensitive Compartmented Information (SCI) cocoon between 1955 and mid-1960, fewer than 350 individuals, including the Lockheed designers, maintenance personnel, and pilots, knew about the U-2 and its actual mission. Known to these few as Aquatone, when overflight operations approached in 1956, it was subsumed in the Talent access and control system, an SCI compartment whose imagery products were separated into two additional access-limited compartments called Chess (European Theater) and Churchdoor (Asian Theater). Indeed, the Sensint and Talent programs were so closely held that neither ever appeared in the deliberations of the National Security Council— not at least until the U-2 "tore its britches," as one participant phrased it, in May 1960 and thereby acquired the unwanted international attention that these missions risked.

The President approved each U-2 mission, and the first two flights over the Soviet Union occurred on 4 and 5 July 1956, when U–2s flew over Leningrad and Moscow, respectively, among other regions of European Russia. The last flight, however, ended rather more dramatically when, on 1 May 1960, the Soviet Union shot down a U-2 deep inside its territory. The resulting international furor mightily embarrassed the administration. The President at first offered a "plausible denial" (a weather research airplane over Turkey had strayed off course)—a cover story that collapsed after the Soviets produced the pilot and charged him with espionage. The U-2 shoot down also ended a Summit Conference almost before it began, with Soviet leaders demanding a personal apology from Eisenhower, one that was not forthcoming. Nevertheless, Eisenhower announced publicly that the United States would not, in the future, conduct clandestine aerial overflights of the Soviet Union, a pledge that he and his successors would keep.

Fortunately for the United States, Eisenhower's earth orbiting strategic reconnaissance satellites succeeded aerial overflights a few months later, beginning successful operations on 18 August 1960. On 25 August, Eisenhower approved the formation of a new office that would control operations of the Air Force satellite Project Samos. Air Force Secretary Dudley C. Sharp issued the requisite organizational directives at the end of the month. The new reconnaissance satellite office, called the Office of Missile and Satellite Systems, a name later shortened to Office of Space Systems, within the Office of the Secretary of the Air Force, would be directed by Air Force Under Secretary Joseph Charyk, who in this capacity reported directly to Secretary of Defense Thomas S. Gates. A special projects office on the West Coast, headed by an Air Force flag officer and responsible for the Samos project, reported directly to Charyk. This action removed the "regular" Air Force from any direct role in American reconnaissance satellites for the remainder of the twentieth century.

With the CIA-Air Force team's Corona producing images, and with Samos separated from the regular Air Force, on 26 August the president sent a memorandum to the secretaries of state and defense, the attorney general, the chairman of the atomic energy commission, and the DCI that announced a new Talent-Keyhole security control system that strictly limited access to reconnaissance satellite products and activities, as well as controlling the flow of that information. "Within your agency," Eisenhower told its recipients, "you shall be personally responsible for the selection of those personnel who will have access to the [reconnaissance satellite] information and for determining the scope of that access. Access is to be on a 'Must-know' basis related to major national security needs."* Underscoring his concern for "Must-know" and the strict need to limit access to this new SCI control system, the president directed that the addressees and each member of his staff cleared for Talent-Keyhole initial the memorandum to signify that they had read it. Corona's photographic images, or "product," later would be separated into another compartment within Talent-Keyhole, called Ruff, which would remain in effect until the Corona program itself concluded in 1972.

President Eisenhower introduced technical intelligence collection from satellites to the Intelligence Community, and in so doing he created for the United States an intelligence revolution. The United States established the National Reconnaissance Office in September 1961 to carry out the revolutionary program of intelligence collection from space. For nearly thirty years thereafter, a small elite staff would assist the Director of the National Reconnaissance Office in building, managing, and improving revolutionary national reconnaissance satellites.

R. Cargill Hall
Former NRO Chief Historian

---

*   Eisenhower, Dwight D., Memorandum for the Secretary of State, The Secretary of Defense, The Attorney General, the Chairman, Atomic Energy Commission, and the Director of Central Intelligence, 26 August 1960.

4C-1000

During the period addressed in this history, the existence of the NRO was a deeply classified fact. When people referred to it at the unclassified level, they often substituted the term "4C-1000" for the name. For example, someone might say, "You need to coordinate this with 4C-1000," or someone at a meeting might say, "I'm from 4C-1000."

4C-1000, also occasionally referred to as "The Suite" by insiders, was actually the Pentagon office where the NRO Deputy Director, the Staff Director, and most of the Staff members were housed. It was located on the 4th floor, C ring, room 1000 — or in Pentagon speak, room 4C-1000. In the early years, the C corridor was open between the 9th and 10th corridors, and the Staff members were in offices along that ring with numbers like 4C-952 or 4C-1026. The Office of the Deputy Director and Staff Director was at the bend in the corridor (room 4C-1000). In 1977, a construction project blocked off the C ring between corridors 9 and 10, and the entire area was opened up as a secure compartmented facility. From then on, the entire area was labeled room 4C-1000, a euphemism for the NRO Staff.

The Director of the NRO occupied one of the E ring offices between corridors 8 and 9 overlooking the River Entrance to the Pentagon. The specific office depended on whether the DNRO was also the Secretary, Under Secretary, or Assistant Secretary of the Air Force. Thus, his office was essentially around the corner from the Staff office space.

In addition to the 4C-1000 area, the Staff also had office spaces in the basement of the Pentagon. This area, Pentagon room BD-944 (basement, D ring, room 944), was a vault that initially housed the Satellite Operations Center (SOC). After the SOC was disestablished in 1977, the space was used by organizations such as NRO TENCAP and the Defense Support Program Office staff. There was a five-flight stairway that ran from the 4th floor on E Ring to the basement, often referred to by Staff members running up and down the stairs as "the heart attack route."

Chapter 1

INTRODUCTION

I am honored to write the introductory chapter to this history of the National Reconnaissance Office (NRO) Staff. I consider my first tour in the NRO, as a field grade officer, to be extraordinarily important, as it gave me a breadth of unique experience and strong understanding of national security space. Later, when I was a brand-new general officer, I was privileged to return as leader of the Staff. Moreover, the relationships and friendships made during those tours continue to the day.

General Thomas S. Moorman Jr., USAF (Ret.)

The National Reconnaissance Office was established in 1961 to manage the National Reconnaissance Program (NRP) in developing, acquiring, and operating the country's satellite reconnaissance systems. The creation of this organization was driven by President Eisenhower's determination that the United States would never again be surprised by "another Pearl Harbor." The mission was of the highest priority. The technology, the intelligence collected, and even the existence of the organization, were highly classified. The organization was led by a Director (DNRO) and the reconnaissance systems were developed and operated by program offices—Program A (Air Force), Program B (Central Intelligence Agency), Program C (Navy), and until 1974, there was a Program D, a joint effort of the CIA and Air Force that developed strategic reconnaissance aircraft. The NRO was supported by a relatively small staff at the outset, growing to about 70, including administrative staff. The basic organizational structure of the NRO remained relatively constant for nearly 30 years.

Over time there have been both classified and unclassified histories written about the NRO and the extraordinary systems that have been built by the program offices. However, there has not been a comprehensive account of the role of the Staff over the organization's first 30 years. This monograph addresses that gap. During the first thirty years of the NRO, the small NRO Staff played an outsized role in the success of the NRO's national reconnaissance programs.

Understanding the role of the NRO Staff begins with an understanding of staff responsibilities. First and foremost, the Staff directly supported the DNRO, a senior political appointee in the Air Force. Another major function of the Staff was to represent the institutional interests of the NRO, especially in the Washington arena. Said a different way, the Staff did its best to try to insulate the program offices from external influences and pressures, so that these offices could concentrate on the mission. The Staff provided the interface to its stakeholders in space policy entities, the oversight structure, the Intelligence Community (IC), the military services, and the civil and commercial space sectors. This does not give a complete picture of the role of the NRO Staff, thus requiring a more complete historical account.

1

To my knowledge, this history is a somewhat unique undertaking, as the activities of a staff are generally considered strictly a support function whose responsibilities are secondary to the operation and execution of the line organization's mission. In the period covered by this history, there were significant technological and environmental changes that affected the NRO:

- New reconnaissance system developments and the associated program office competition.

- Significant budget growth.

- Expansion from a strictly strategic orientation to include tactical support to military operations.

- Increase in oversight, especially with the creation of the congressional intelligence committees.

- Turmoil in the launch area, with the NRO programs changing from expendable rockets to the Space Shuttle and back to expendables.

- The general "whitening"—emergence and awareness—of the NRO.

Reviewing how the Staff dealt with these and other challenges is not only an interesting story but also is essential to understanding the evolution of the NRO. Additionally, this history can provide lessons-learned that could be useful for managing other very high priority, time-sensitive, technology-driven programs.

There is also an important human dimension to this narrative. The Staff's ability to handle these challenges was due in no small part to the streamlined management authorities afforded to the NRO because of the criticality of the mission. A critical element of this streamlined management was selective manning where each Staff member was handpicked, and the tours of duty were stable. Thus, the capabilities of the people were remarkable. The organization had a short decision cycle with ready access to leadership. Each individual was considered an expert on his or her program, and staffers were empowered to act. It is important to underscore that, given the scope of their responsibilities, these individuals were relatively junior compared to other organizations with similar responsibilities. As a side note, people who served on the Staff were highly successful in their later government assignments and with industry.

This introduction would not be complete without acknowledging the role of Colonel Phil Datema, USAF (Ret.) in making this history a reality. He was the one who recognized the need to document this story. Without his tireless efforts and dogged persistence over many years, the monograph would not have been published. I would also like to thank Dr. Bob McDonald (Director Emeritus of the Center for the Study of National Reconnaissance) and his staff for their research and editorial support.

General Thomas S. Moorman Jr., USAF (Ret.)
NRO Staff Director, 1985-87
Commander, USAF Space Command, 1990-92
Vice Chief of Staff, USAF, 1994-97

Chapter 2

THEMES

During the course of researching for this history, a number of recurring themes were found. While these themes were not individually unique to the NRO Staff, the collection as a whole distinguishes the NRO Staff from most other government staff organizations. These distinguishing themes begin to answer the question, "Why would one undertake writing a history some 30 years after the organization was assimilated into a much larger, restructured National Reconnaissance Office?" What were the unique characteristics of this staff organization, referred to simply as "4C-1000," the Pentagon office of this highly covert staff organization during most of its existence? We will briefly highlight these key themes in this chapter, providing supportive detail in the following sections.

> **Theme 1:** CRITICALITY AND SENSITIVITY — The criticality and sensitivity of the NRO mission drove the need for special security, which was enabled by streamlined management processes, a hallmark of the NRO.

The NRO was created by President Eisenhower in response to his conviction that the United States should never experience another Pearl Harbor—this during a time when America's visibility into its dominant threat, the Soviet Union, was at best, limited. This critical national threat called for an unconventional organization, with unconventional security and management processes removing many of the checks and balances characteristic of conventional programs and organizations. Essential to success, this critical and sensitive mission had to be recognized by those at every government level.

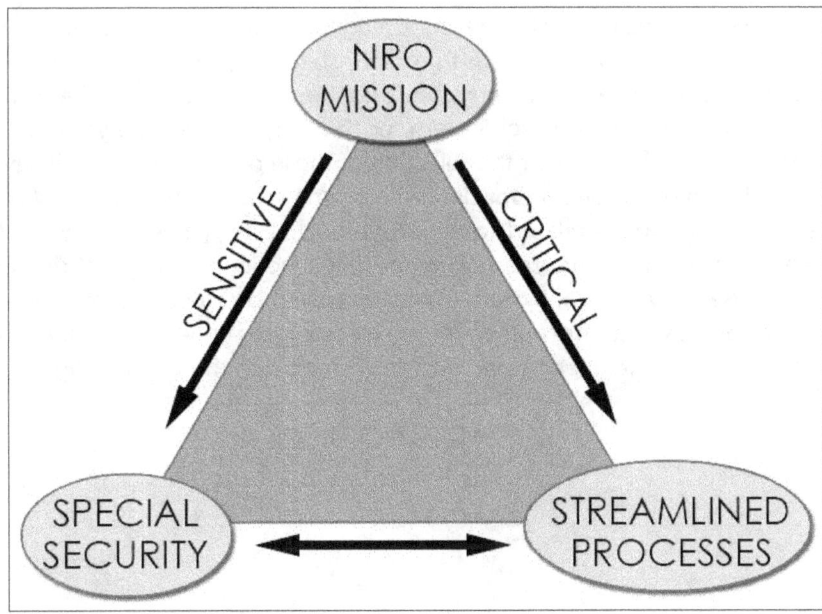

3

NRO Mission

The National Reconnaissance Program was a single program, national in character, to meet the intelligence needs of the Government under a strong national leadership, for the development, management, control, and cooperation of all the projects, both current and long range, for the collection of intelligence and mapping and geodetic information obtained through overflights (excluding peripheral reconnaissance operations). The potentialities of U.S. technology and all operational resources and facilities must be aggressively and imaginatively exploited to develop and operate systems for the collection of intelligence which are fully responsive to the Government's intelligence needs and objectives.[1] Key words here are *"single program, national...all projects...for collection of intelligence...through overflights [satellite and airborne]."*[2] The sensitivity and criticality of the NRO mission drove the need for special security and streamlined processes at every level in executing the National Reconnaissance Program.

Special Security

As unusual as it might be for a President to sign written instructions to Cabinet officers regarding the need for secrecy and security practices, President Eisenhower emphasized the importance of the content of security "indoctrination" briefings, or initial security instructions, at the time of first exposure to this class of information. He directed that every individual be approved and briefed on the fragility and sensitivity of the information, as well as their protection obligations. As a result, those Presidential instructions were implemented by the NRO and other components of the Intelligence Community by policies, practices, and procedures that rigorously applied the requirement to diligently ensure individuals were qualified for access, to restrict the need for "Must-know" decision authority, to disclose details of the NRP only to the level required for specific operations or required support, and to manage carefully the flow of information that would potentially expose the NRP or inhibit its operational efficiency and mission effectiveness. The NRO security staff was the Director of Central Intelligence (DCI)'s and DNRO's executive agent for orchestrating and overseeing execution of the President's and DCI's security direction in the NRO and Executive Branch.

> I hereby direct that the products of satellite reconnaissance, and information of the fact of such reconnaissance revealed by this product, shall be given strict security handling under the provisions of a special security control system approved by me. I hereby approve the Talent-Keyhole Security Control System for this purpose...Within your agency, you shall be personally responsible for the selection of those personnel who will have access to the foregoing information and for determining the scope of that access. Access is to be on a "must know" basis related to major national security needs.... When they are indoctrinated, they shall be informed of my specific direction to them that the provisions of the special Security Control System I have approved be strictly complied with...the responsibility for the selection of personnel may be delegated only to the senior intelligence chief or chiefs within the agencies serving as members of the U.S. Intelligence Board.[3]
>
> —Dwight D. Eisenhower
> 26 August 1960

This memorandum, signed by the President one year before the creation of the National Reconnaissance Office, set the tone, invoking the Talent-Keyhole (TK) security control system in limiting the exposure of the "fact of" and details of satellite reconnaissance. The Talent control system was created in the mid-1950s for the U-2 and other airborne reconnaissance programs. It was expanded in 1960 to the Talent-Keyhole control system to protect the products of satellite reconnaissance systems. Incidentally, it can be argued that with President Eisenhower's 1960 memo in which he personally controlled the access approval process, the White House, not the Central Intelligence Agency or Department of Defense (DoD), virtually assumed ownership of the Talent-Keyhole security control system.

This fundamental recognition of the importance of overhead reconnaissance and the need to maintain the covert nature of the NRO, and the systems it managed, drove *everything*. Security management was the first priority to protect the country's capabilities so that adversaries could not deny or deceive the nation. The need for security permeated everything and dictated how the enterprise was organized and staffed, as well as how projects were acquired and operated. For example, the enterprise enjoyed the highest defense supply chain priority, called "Brickbat 1." Exercising this priority could demand support from any national security or industrial base entity. Speed and responsiveness to needs were judged essential. This led to the highly streamlined decision chain that included a flat staff structure and a waiver of much of the staff oversight that would be normal for programs of the magnitude and importance of those managed by the NRO. There was a willingness to accept more than the normal financial and technical risk to achieve rapid results and security.

Examples of NRO Streamlined Management[4]

As a national organization, the NRO is integrated and interagency-manned by highly qualified personnel motivated by their NRP mission to provide the necessary objectivity to their decision makers. Historically, the program has been marked by a high stability of personnel manning, which has been beneficial to continuity and effectiveness. This stability stems from the high program priority.

- The DNRO…has resource allocation authority within a fenced budget. This provides…budget flexibility.

- The DNRO has direct access to his line organization elements. This short vertical up and down chain makes his programs highly responsive and makes him directly accessible to his program managers.

- The DNRO controls end-to-end system contracting and procedures which, therefore, makes it responsive.

- The NRP enjoys strict internal review by select audit organizations and personnel. This limits indiscriminate reviews by any number of agencies that might feel a necessity to intervene in NRP matters.

The special security required for collection system protection provides a management spin-off by allowing conduct of NRP system acquisition, conduct, and operations in, essentially, a sanctuary environment. This environment prevents unwarranted external intrusion into NRP activities.

5

Toward the end of the Staff's history, however, the mission of the NRO became less critical from a standpoint of national survival and less sensitive due to general acceptance of satellite reconnaissance. The Iron Curtain was eroding, and the risk of catastrophic surprise was no longer an overriding threat. With a number of authorized and unauthorized disclosures, the NRO mission had also lost much of its sensitivity, and all of this impacted the Staff. Accordingly, NRO Directors Edward ("Pete") Aldridge and Martin Faga each initiated internal studies, initially conducted by the NRO Staff, which ultimately led to declassifying the fact of the NRO's existence and limited details of the Office in 1992.[5] The Byeman security system was later replaced to allow for more reasonable processes for balancing protection and disclosure of program information.

Streamlined Processes

More than a guiding principle, streamlined management was directed by the early founders of the National Reconnaissance Program. In a memo from Roswell L. Gilpatric, the Deputy Secretary of Defense, to Allen W. Dulles, Director of Central Intelligence, Gilpatric directed, "Within the Department of Defense, the Department of the Air Force will be the operational agency for management and conduct of the NRP, and will conduct this program through use of *streamlined special management procedures* involving direct control from the Office of the Secretary of the Air Force to Reconnaissance System Project Directors in the field, without intervening reviews or approval."[6]

The following summer, the Director of the NRO Joseph V. Charyk assigned responsibility to the NRO Staff in assisting the DNRO in establishing and maintaining effective streamlined management procedures appropriate to the mission of the NRO and consistent with the security considerations which apply, stating:

> The NRO will be kept as small as possible in order to operate with the efficiency and quick reaction time required. The Office will consist of carefully selected personnel of the highest qualifications and will be confined to the minimum number required to accomplish the task under the conditions which apply. By arranging these personnel so that other, larger groups may be controlled through overt (additional duty) assignments of NRO Program Directors, the actual size of the NRO may be kept quite small, and thus more easily concealed, although the size of the personnel and resources directly controlled (in industry, for example) is necessarily large.[7]

The NRO was granted a great deal of flexibility in budget planning and execution. From inception, it incrementally funded the satellite programs, avoiding large budget variations from year to year. This also enabled it to modify satellites in development to take advantage of advancing technologies or address evolving requirements. It also had the authority to carry forward any unspent budget from year to year. These authorities provided flexibility to address satellite failures in response to urgent requirements without the need to request a "new start" authority, supplemental funding or a reprogramming action, or to lose unspent budget due to expiring funds. The NRO's budget was reviewed and approved through a very streamlined process.

A four-person NRP Executive Committee (EXCOM)* had authority to authorize new programs or modifications to existing programs without further review within the executive branch. Congressional review was limited to the Armed Forces Committee Chairs and staff directors in each house.

Beginning in the mid-1970s, the NRO faced its greatest challenges to its streamlined practices from external sources, including Congress and an expanding user base. According to Martin Faga, former NRO Staff member and NRO Director, "The expanded user base meant more stakeholders seeking service from the NRO and the need for more requirements setting and active budgeting by the DCI. The NRO budget escalated, reaching a peak in the mid-80s."[8]

> "The whole idea was to keep (the NRO) streamlined." It was created in response to an urgent crisis. "We didn't need or want to go through many channels to achieve our goals. We needed to make decisions promptly and not worry about the bureaucracy."
>
> — Dr. Joseph Charyk,
> 26 September 2014

Despite external challenges to NRO Staff streamlined practices with adjustments in its management process, the NRO continued to function efficiently in comparison to conventional government staff organizations during the mid- to late 1970s and early 1980s. For example, the NRO Staff continued to practice selective manning and retention of key personnel. Staff members were empowered by leadership, often representing the NRO at White House, Congressional, and Intelligence Community forums. Special security procedures were quickly developed, relying primarily on accountability and best judgment, rather than a set of rules. Staff growth was minimized.

Finally, in the late 1980s, streamlined processes, long the hallmark of the NRO, began to give way to normalization, a necessary response due to the NRO's changing external environment, which is the subject of the following chapter.

Theme 2: AGILITY AND ADAPTABILITY — The NRO Staff rapidly adapted to the changing environment (e.g., threat, technology, oversight, and employment, as well as internal demands for decision support).

The NRO, during the years that the Staff existed, was in a nearly continual state of change. It started as a highly covert organization with only a few senior leaders aware of its existence, and its systems had short lives and served only a few, but very important, intelligences purposes. By 1990, the organization managed a large array of highly capable and long-lived satellite systems that served nearly every intelligence need and were essential for the conduct of military operations. Throughout that transition, the Staff was instrumental to the NRO's successful adaption to the changing environment.

---

*   The EXCOM, established in August 1965, "reduced the authority of the Director [of the NRO], transferring many of the rights and responsibilities [to] three voting (and one non-voting) members: the Deputy Secretary of Defense, the Director of Central Intelligence, the Special Assistant to the President for Science and Technology, and (non-voting) the Director, National Reconnaissance Office…The functions allocated to the National Reconnaissance Program were in many respects defined more clearly than those assigned in earlier [instructions]….It was not all that clear however, whether the National Reconnaissance Office had sufficient authority to exercise those functions. [A History of Satellite Reconnaissance, Robert L. Perry, p. 73]

7

In that capacity, the Staff had to deal with all the changes that drove increased complexity. The chart below provides a visual picture of how this complexity increased over time.

TIME	Early Years	Middle Years	Later Years
	1962-1974	1974-1980	1980-1990
COMPLEXITY	• Technology push • Primarily strategic users • EXCOM/minimal oversight • Single mission, space-centric architectures • Restricted industrial base	• More capable systems • Budget constraints • DoD/DCI priority conflicts • Increased oversight in both Executive & Legislative branches • Expanding user base • ASAT Threat • Spies & security compromises • Increasing use of shared infrastructure (e.g. STS) • Priority debates	• Complex, multi-system architectures • Increased support to military users • More capable systems • *Challenger* loss and shuttle recovery • Increased oversight • Expanding user base • DARPA/SDIO space initiatives • Government Continuity and Survivability issues • Internal competition

This complexity was driven by a number of factors:

Advances in Technology. In the early years of the NRO, the limitations were technical, the acquisition contracts sole-source, the satellites short-lived, and the users important, but few. Continual advances in technology led to much more capable and long-lived satellite systems which cost more, required longer development timelines, and forced trades among potential new capabilities. This also led to more industrial competition and more people with a need to know about the NRO and its system capabilities.

Expanding User Community. At the beginning, the user community was small, and the focus was on avoiding technological surprise and addressing some key intelligence issues for the nuclear planning community. As capabilities improved, the number of users and tasks increased. Some of the most consequential missions were treaty monitoring and support to

8

military operations (SMO). These increased uses greatly expanded the number of people cleared for and involved with NRO systems.

Expanding Management and Oversight. Early on, oversight and programmatic decisions were held at the principle levels in the national security community. The DNRO took direction from the Secretary of Defense (SECDEF) and requirements from the United States Intelligence Board (USIB). Other government staff elements were not cleared to know of the existence of the NRO, and Congress dealt with the programs at the level of committee chairmen and ranking members. As the budget increased and decisions became more consequential, the amount of staff involvement, both in the executive and congressional branches, continually increased, and DNRO decisions became subject to much broader review.

Increasing Competition for Collection Resources. Initially, operational tasking was provided by US Intelligence Board committees that met several times a month. As system capabilities grew and the number and diversity of users increased, more inclusive requirements, tasking, and funding mechanisms had to be established. Support to Military Operations was a particular challenge that resulted in numerous institutionalized outreach efforts, new programmatic vehicles, new offices within the services, NRO system experimentation, and extensive staff interactions.

> "This is the personal staff of the DNRO where the DNRO over time confronted vastly different situations. He and his staff had to adjust…and they did."
>
> — Martin Faga,
> Former DNRO

Increasing Interagency and System Interfaces. When first organized, the NRO relied on the United States Air Force (USAF) to provide launch services and satellite control services through the Air Force Satellite Control Facility, but was otherwise largely self-sufficient. Over time, the number of technical and programmatic interfaces between the NRO and other government agencies increased. The collaboration on the Space Shuttle was the most significant, but there were other coordinated programs and relationships, all of which required intensive coordination and negotiation.

9

The DNRO, supported by the NRO Staff, constituted the "Headquarters NRO." The individual program offices concurrently executed the NRP while also maintaining close relationships with their home organizations, the Air Force, the CIA, and the Navy. This often led NRO stakeholders to view the NRO as a confederation of semi-independent program offices, each with separate reporting channels. Thus, one of the key roles of the NRO Staff was to support and promote an *integrated* National Reconnaissance Program.

> **Theme 3:** REPRESENTATION AND ADVOCACY — The NRO Staff was a small, empowered organization that aggressively engaged across the US government and industry to ensure that the NRP could be successfully executed.

With the exception of security, the functions the NRO Staff were similar to those performed by any military service staff. The NRO Staff, however, was much smaller by comparison with any other such staff, at most about 70 professionals, including administrative support, and the Staff size did not appreciably change as the complexity of their responsibilities expanded over time. It was a very flat organization. For the most part, it was a young group of professionals—the Staff Director was normally a junior Brigadier General, and the office directors were mid-level military or civilian officers. Each individual was an empowered action officer with direct and frequent access to the Deputy Director (DDNRO) and DNRO.

One of the indicators of continuing streamlined management within the NRO Staff is reflected by the relatively small size of the Staff and its small growth over time. In spite of the increasing number and complexity of NRO programs and the growth of external oversight, the NRO Staff grew from 44 to 70 individuals, or 59% over its 28-year history, compared to a six-fold increase in NRO resources over the same period, when adjusted for inflation.

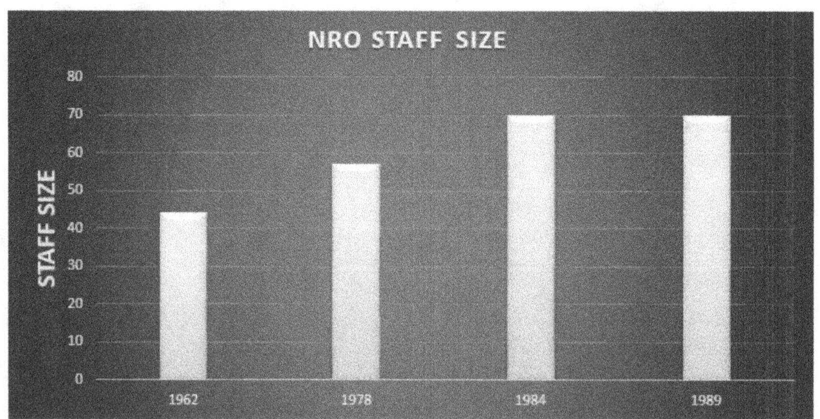

10

The small Staff consistently "punched above its weight." It was not at all uncommon for a junior action officer to interact with counterparts three or four ranks more senior. Staff members were viewed as subject matter experts and were trusted to use their judgment in interactions with other institutions. The action officers frequently interacted directly with the DNRO and DDNRO, both to get direction and to provide feedback on external interactions. Representative interactions included:

- Participating in the continual Washington-area intelligence community forums, which included the Committee on Imagery Requirements and Exploitation (COMIREX),[*] the SIGINT Committee,[†] and the Civil Applications Committee.[‡]

- Supporting the National Security Council (NSC) and proposing policy language that impacted documents subsequently published as Presidential Directives.

- Negotiating interagency agreements with the National Security Agency (NSA), the National Aeronautics and Space Administration (NASA), and others.

- Representing the NRO in IC trade studies and program priority debates.

- Providing support and involvement in all key studies leading to the creation of Air Force Space Command.

- Providing briefings to key decision makers such as the President's Foreign Intelligence Advisory Board (PFIAB), military Combatant Commanders and senior service leaders, and in several instances, the political leader of an allied country that participated in some aspect of satellite reconnaissance.

- Finally, as noted earlier, the Staff provided a single point of contact to the external environment for policy, programmatic, budget, security, program capabilities, and administrative matters.

> "The Staff turned the crank very well, knew how to get the information to Congress, to get the approval, working with the programs and Congress in the allocation process. For example, the *increase in warning time study* was used in the Congressional process and impacted the decision to proceed. The Staff did run the *photo war studies*, almost annually that looked at the impact of adding various capabilities that impacted program decisions. They were effective in leading to the demise of the current photo systems…to show we have a capable replacement."
>
> — Col Dave Raspet, USAF (Ret.),
> former Staff member and Deputy Director, Program A,
> 12 September 2013

---

* COMIREX advised the DCI on collection, processing, and exploitation of imagery, formulated guidance and priorities for mission planning and tasking, and provided interface for R&D of imagery processing and interpretation.

† The SIGINT Committee advised the DCI on the establishment of Sigint requirements, priorities, and objectives, developed guidance on objectives and priorities of collection and on exploitation requirements for Comint, Elint, foreign instrumentation signals, nonimagery infrared, coherent light, and nonnuclear electromagnetic pulse sources. It also monitored and evaluated the responsiveness of present and programmed US and cooperating foreign Sigint resources to U.S. needs for intelligence information.

‡ The Civil Applications Committee was the interagency committee officially chartered in 1975 by the Office of the President to coordinate and provide Federal civil agencies access to National Systems data in support of mission responsibilities.

11

This staff-led approach served three purposes. It protected the program officers of the NRO from being distracted from their acquisition responsibilities by being called to Washington for oversight or user briefings. It provided a conduit from the Staff to the program offices to keep them abreast of issues and opportunities. It also provided a consistent NRO enterprise voice to the external environment.

The Staff also performed some *line* responsibilities that cut across the interests of the program offices. These included:

- Logistics support for the enterprise.

- Security execution and guidance for the enterprise.

- Management of the communications organization that provided dedicated support to the enterprise.

- Managing the NRO Film and Chemistry contract that directed the Eastman Kodak film production and processing efforts.[*]

The Staff also functioned, on occasion, as a special staff to the DNRO in his capacity as either Secretary or Under Secretary of the Air Force (SECAF). One key example is the Staff's extensive role in recovery efforts following the failure of the Space Shuttle *Challenger* and two NRO Titan 34D launch vehicles in the mid-1980s. In that case, Secretary Aldridge leaned on the NRO Staff, bypassing the otherwise cumbersome Pentagon staffing processes, to expedite a return to flight for national security payloads. This is chronicled in greater detail in Chapter 6.

---

[*]   Costs for research and product development of extremely high performance film product were borne by Eastman Kodak, allowing the company to market the products to other customers.

12

Chapter 3

PEOPLE OF THE NRO STAFF

The men and women of the NRO Staff were the foundation of the corporate NRO. In an interview with Dr. Charyk, the first Director of the NRO, he emphasized, "We had to gather a small but very qualified group that knew where to go for information."[9] Staff members were all hand-picked and nominated to the Staff Director. Once selected, individuals typically served two to three years on the Staff before returning to their home offices. For Air Force personnel, this pool of highly talented people was facilitated by assignment selection and retention processes formally controlled by the Air Force Military Personnel Center Special Assignments branch. Other services and government organizations, such as CIA, NSA, and the services had similar processes, yet in every case Staff members served at the pleasure of the Staff Director*. This specialized selection and retention process yielded a talented staff with diversity of experience. However, virtually all former Staff members interviewed stated that the sense of empowerment and allegiance to a common national mission was the most compelling motivation, creating a sense of *esprit de corps* transcending program and home office allegiances.

> "The NRO staff was comprised of technical, highly knowledgeable people… otherwise, you just had a staff."
>
> — Dr. Joseph Charyk,
> Former DNRO

The NRO Staff evolved from the Missile and Satellite Office which had been established in 1960 to support Dr. Charyk as manager of the Air Force SAMOS program. This pre-NRO Staff, led by Brig Gen Richard D. Curtin, chief of the Missiles and Space Systems Office, was predominantly an Air Force staff with token Army and Navy representation.[10] The Air Force continued to provide the majority of personnel to the NRO Staff throughout the Staff's history.

Dr. Richard M. Bissel, Jr.
Co-Director NRO: 6 Sep 1961 - 28 Feb 1962

Dr. Joseph V. Charyk
Co-Director NRO: 6 Sep 1961 - 28 Feb 1962
DNRO: 1 Mar 1962 - 28 Feb 1963

---

*   The NRO Staff Director served as the reviewing or endorsing official on all performance reports.

13

The founding co-director of the NRO, Dr. Richard Bissell, Jr., continued to operate with his own staff from CIA headquarters and did not believe CIA officers should be assigned to the NRO Staff,[11] although early DNROs, including Charyk and McMillan, urged senior CIA leadership to provide greater representation to the NRO Staff.[12] From its inception, the NRO Staff was composed of individuals who were nominated for the position by a sponsor from within the cleared community and were then accepted by the Staff Director, DDNRO, or DNRO. Often there was a negotiation between the program offices and the NRO leadership to determine who was assigned and for how long they served. The early Staff also recruited from the military services, most notably the Army and Navy to represent Army and Navy interests in space. Throughout its history, the NRO Staff included representatives from the services' operational and intelligence communities, as well as defense and national organizations such as the Defense Mapping Agency (DMA), the National Security Agency, and NASA. Over time, the preponderance of Staff personnel came from those already assigned to the NRO program offices.

Robert Pattishall, former Staff member and Program B Signals Intelligence (Sigint) program manager, observed a significant transformation in the priority of CIA resourcing for the NRO Staff following the cancelation of a large Sigint program in the late 1970s.

Despite folklore to the contrary, the consensus among Staff members was that their allegiance was to the DNRO, and hence the Staff Director, rather than the program office from which they had been assigned. Rick Buckley, the Director of Systems and Technology in the late 1980s stated:

> The selection process (in my case) was primarily with Julian Caballero, the CIA Director of Program B in conjunction with the Staff Director, Brig Gen Tom Moorman.... I interviewed with Brig Gen Moorman, and was selected. Both Bob Kohler and Julian Caballero said that I would be working for Jimmie Hill, Pete Aldridge, and Tom Moorman, (not for Program B), and both said, "If you need anything, let us know, and otherwise we won't bother you.[13]

That is not to say there were not infractions, individual cases in which people represented individual or program biases, but these cases were the exception and were dealt with accordingly. One Program Element Monitor (PEM), for example, was replaced on the Staff when he knowingly briefed a congressional staffer on a program position that was contrary to the NRO Director's position. According to former DNRO Martin Faga, "It would be inappropriate to frame the incident as typical. This was the exception rather than the rule, even though the Staff Program Element Monitors always had dual responsibilities…to the program office and to the Staff. They were supposed to get the conversation framed for the leadership. They were to keep both sides informed."[14]

The characteristic most commonly attributed to NRO Staff members was that of *empowerment*. Martin Faga noted that Staff members typically "punched above their weight," performing above their pay grades or position in an organizational chart.[15] The following is just one of the many, often personal, examples that were cited during the interview process for this project that point to the level of trust and confidence enjoyed by members of the Staff. Similar stories were repeated by virtually every individual interviewed for this history.

Mr. Martin C. Faga
DNRO: 28 Sep 1989 - 5 Mar 1993

"As young action officers, we had huge authority and responsibility on the NRO Staff. I got a call on Friday that I had to go to the White House Situation Room and brief Carlucci [the National Security Advisor] and some guy named Powell [soon to be the Assistant to the President for National Security Affairs – APNSA – and eventually Chairman of the Joint Chiefs of Staff]….on [a proposed new] program. It was going to be on Tuesday. I worked all weekend [to modify the charts] and then went to Jimmie Hill and asked if he wanted to see the slides. His answer to me was, what for? Well, before I go to Mr. Aldridge to show him the slides, he [says] he doesn't want to see them. So, as a young major or lieutenant colonel, I went to the Situation Room of the White House to brief Carlucci and Powell on the program without any review. It was amazing the amount of trust the senior managers, the senior decision makers in the NRO, had in their young staff officers."[16]

— Col Gary Dahlen, USAF (Ret.),
NRO Staff R&D Manager, 1985-1990

Much of this *esprit de corps* was derived from being minimally supervised, maximally empowered, and imbued with a sense of elitism—yet still accountable.

A down-side of this sense of empowerment was a view held by many outsiders, particularly in the Air Force, that NRO officers were "prima donnas," or part of the "Hollywood Air Force," rather than the mainstream Air Force. Robert Perry, in his account of the early days of the NRO, observed:

> Much of the Air Staff…looked on the NRO as a not-quite-respectable collection of Air Force dissenters under the thumb of the CIA. Air Force officers who were wholly loyal to their NRO responsibilities sometimes felt that the "regular" Air Force had cast them out. At least one CIA staffer seconded to the NRO found himself effectively frozen out of his parent organization because of his stubborn adherence to the spirit as well as the letter of the NRO charter. Some Air Force officers may have felt the same way when the time came for them to move from an NRO assignment to another in the regular service. For Air Force and Agency personnel, to be assigned to the NRO in any capacity, particularly in the troubled days between 1963 and 1966, was not uniformly looked on as a wholly happy circumstance.[17]

This negative view declined somewhat over time, but it was exasperated by the "hand-selection" process and blanket travel orders and the fact that NRO military officers were generally discouraged, and often restricted, from wearing military uniforms. This "uniform issue" was often the source of considerable consternation among senior officers in the Pentagon who discovered they were dealing with junior officers on a matter, rather than with a mid- or relatively high-level NRO civilian.[18]

Follow-on career assignments were often "by-name" postings to other organizations that were involved with other aspects of the NRO's activities. Many returned to a home program office. Some were posted to high-level staff jobs, including those in the Office of the Secretary of Defense (OSD), the IC Staff, and the White House. Others returned to the Intelligence Community or services as part of the user base that they supported, most often as stronger advocates of NRO programs and policies.

15

Chapter 4

EXTERNAL ENVIRONMENT

At its inception, the number of people cleared to even know of the existence of the NRO was extremely limited. The programs were focused on avoiding technological surprise and supporting national strategic planning. The stakeholder community, likewise, was small. Decisions were largely made through discussions and letters among principal actors (e.g. the DNRO, SECDEF, CIA Director, and the President's National Security Advisor). These principals had very few staff members cleared to support them. Reconnaissance satellite performance was limited in those days more by technology, than by financial resources. Congress had a very limited role with respect to the Intelligence Community, the National Reconnaissance Office in particular. As described by former NRO historian Clayton Laurie:

> The history of the NRO's interaction with Congress is closely intertwined with the security demands of the Cold War, the growth and development of the Intelligence Community as a whole, and with the American Space program. In that setting, the novel relationship between the NRP and Congress has undergone significant changes over 50 years, and it continues to evolve as each institution addresses the nation's intelligence demands and post-Cold War security challenges of the twenty-first century.[19]

The early issues the NRO Staff had to deal with were generally internally driven and involved supporting the DNRO's assessment of technical and design risk and his needs relative to the internal organizational debates.

Externally, by 1990, the number of people cleared to know about the NRO and its programs had grown exponentially, numbering in several thousands. The programs were supporting a range of technical, strategic, and military operational requirements. They were complex and expensive and included space, ground, and user components. There were far more requirements than funds available, and that led to numerous trade studies and funding debates. Both the DoD and the Intelligence Community had extensive staffs involved in program assessments and oversight functions. The decision process also involved staff elements from an expanding number of stakeholders (intelligence agencies, military organizations, civil agencies, and Congress). The industrial base included dozens of companies and much more competition. By this time, the issues the Staff dealt with were primarily externally driven and involved interacting with all the management staff and stakeholder players, as well as engaging with and keeping the program offices informed, while shielding them from the day-to-day Washington issues.

The purpose of this chapter is not to restate history. Rather, it is to provide a quick reference for some of the geopolitical factors that most impacted the Staff role as it evolved from its inception through 1990 when the NRO began transitioning more towards a traditional "three-letter" Defense agency.

17

The Early Years—Kennedy, Johnson, and Nixon Administrations (1962-1974)

External Factors. The dominating national security drivers during this time were strategic—the Cold War rivalry, deterrence, intelligence needed for SIOP* planning, and risks posed to the balance of power by technological surprise. At the same time, there was an urgent need to replace U-2-derived intelligence following Francis Gary Powers' shootdown, coupled with satellites entering early operation. An overriding Presidential concern was to avoid any public disclosure of overhead reconnaissance that could create a serious national security incident.

This sense of urgency and security led to establishing the NRO as a deeply covert activity, and that urgency drove all the streamlined management aspects of the NRO Staff, including its own small size and paucity of intermediate levels, the lack of oversight staffs, and the constraints on the number of companies involved.

Details regarding collection programs, the management organization, contractors, budget, and development and acquisition details were separately compartmented from operational employment and product information to maintain a strict need-to-know security system. Debates existed over whether the NRO should be organized with a strong "CEO" (as favored by the DoD) or with strong operating elements and a Director who served as a "Chairman of the Board" (as favored by the CIA). The "CEO" model prevailed with a small corporate staff and the Director making major decisions on budgets, policy, and program starts.[20]

National Reconnaissance Program Decision Process. The internal NRO decision and NRP budget process was informal and largely accomplished through discussions and letters among the principals. The assignment of responsibility for development of a next generation imagery system (Hexagon) was controversial, with both the Air Force (Program A) and the CIA (Program B) competing to lead the program. The external NRP decision process, on the other hand, was more structured in the early years. The Executive Committee was established in 1965 to facilitate NRP decision making. At a higher level, the EXCOM met quarterly to review progress and approve the budget. The EXCOM's membership varied over time, but the Deputy Secretary of Defense served as Chairman, and the members included the DCI and the Special Assistant to the President for Science and Technology (soon replaced by the President's National Security Advisor). The EXCOM formed sub-committees to address specific issues and invited the participation of intelligence agencies, including the National Security Agency, the Defense Intelligence Agency (DIA), and others serving on the US Intelligence Board. The DNRO served as the Executive Secretary and was responsible for establishing the agenda, presenting information, making recommendations, and documenting decisions.

The EXCOM addressed a number of other NRP issues, such as internal NRO and EXCOM debates over the best path to proceed toward near real-time imagery, with Program A and the DNRO (Dr. McLucas) proposing a film-based solution (Film Readout Gambit or FROG) and Program B proposing a more advanced but higher risk near real-time Electro-Optical Imagery (EOI) solution. The EXCOM in this instance took no position, but it approved funding for research for film readout systems. The NRO Staff R&D funds for readout systems were managed by the NRO Staff.[21] The decision was ultimately made by the President, based upon the recommendation of the Land Committee, selecting the higher risk, but more advanced and capable EOI technical solution.[22]

---

   *   Strategic Air Command's Single Integrated Operational Plan (Initially presented to President Kennedy in 1962).

18

In another instance, intelligence uncertainties regarding the strategic threat posed by the USSR's development of the SA-5, which at the time was believed to be an anti-ballistic missile (ABM) system, led to Programs A and B proposing three different technical approaches to better understand the threat. The EXCOM, after consideration, chose to fund all three.* Such decisions demonstrated the extent to which decision makers at that time prioritized mission success much more than cost.

International Events. There were a number of international events during the early years that impacted the NRO, and hence the NRO Staff. The Cuban Missile Crisis of October 1962, only weeks after the creation of the NRO Staff, highlighted the need for strategic reconnaissance — in this case to monitor events less than 100 miles from the US mainland. Similarly, the Arab-Israeli Six Day War in June 1967, the Warsaw Pact invasion of Czechoslovakia in August 1968, and the Yom Kipper War in October 1973, all created increasing pressure for development of near real-time imagery systems. Similarly, Soviet deployment of mobile intercontinental ballistic missiles (ICBMs) in 1976 generated Strategic Air Command (SAC) requirements for responsive NRP capabilities. Finally, a 1968 incident involving an airborne overflight of Vietnam contributed to the eventual termination of the NRO's airborne program with assets either retired or transferred to the Air Force in 1974.

Congress. In the early years, only a few Congressional committee chairmen and virtually no congressional staff were cleared to know about the NRO and satellite reconnaissance operations. According to NRO historian Clayton Laurie, "As long as the NRO's intelligence product satisfied national command authorities, those few in Congress who were witting asked very few questions about satellite system architecture, funding, management practices, or day-to-day operations." [23] Congressional interactions remained at the principals' level with only Committee Chairmen and Ranking Members of oversight and budget committees briefed on the programs.

Key Policy and Treaties. The Staff included a policy function focused on coordinating internal and external policy issues that had implications for the NRO. Its function was to support the DNRO in protecting the organization's interests. One example of this was the Outer Space Treaty that provided the basis for development and codification of international space law. Space was considered a sanctuary because it was viewed as an element of strategic deterrence. The USSR was aware that any interference with space systems would be viewed as an attempt to disable an element of the US strategic deterrent and a precursor to a strategic nuclear attack, and the US would respond accordingly.

Space Transportation System. Development of the Space Shuttle began in the early 1970s, and the NRO was involved nearly from the start. The shuttle program had huge implications for the NRO, involving everything from the size of NRO satellites to the production rate of launch platforms necessary to launch NRO satellites into orbit, not to mention, budgetary impacts.

---

* Jimmie Hill recounted to Jim Beale in a 1979 meeting the 1968 decision to address the SA-5 surface-to-air missile threat by developing each of the three technology approaches under consideration. No one knew which, if any, would answer the intelligence question, but the threat was judged so critical that the decision makers concluded the three technology solutions should be pursued in parallel.

19

The Middle Years—Ford and Carter Administrations (1974-1980)

By the beginning of the Ford Administration, the Cold War and concerns of an imminent strategic engagement had been reduced through diplomacy and treaty agreements. Ensuring against strategic surprise remained a paramount objective, but treaty monitoring and verification had become a driver for the NRO. The Vietnam War and events like the Warsaw Pact invasion of Czechoslovakia demonstrated the need for timely intelligence that could provide both strategic warning and tactical support to military operations. Technology advancements were making such capabilities viable. Broader concerns about intelligence abuses investigated by the Church and Pike Committees led to expanded Congressional oversight and establishment of the House Permanent Select Committee on Intelligence (HPSCI) and the Senate Select Committee on Intelligence (SSCI) with charters that included oversight of the NRO. The executive branch responded with expanded management oversight and staff involvement primarily by the DCI, DoD, and the White House staff. The NRO Staff remained the "front door" for the NRO in its interactions with the external community.

Mr. James W. Plummer
DNRO: 21 Dec 1973 - 28 Jun 1976

Escalating Oversight. Intelligence abuses and reform was a major issue. President Ford and later President Reagan issued Executive Orders on intelligence oversight that included recognition of "special offices for collection of specialized intelligence through reconnaissance programs"—a euphemism that was intended for the NRP and other "special programs."[24] As previously mentioned, the EXCOM, a streamlined highly centralized Executive body for managing community programs and resources, was terminated in 1976 and replaced briefly by the Committee for Foreign Intelligence. The oversight process became much more "decentralized," seemingly changing to a broader look by people at a lower level.[25] The Church and Pike Committees identified intelligence abuses that led to establishment of the HPSCI and SSCI, with budget and program oversight of all intelligence activities including the NRO. The DCI created the Intelligence Community Staff (IC Staff) which included analysis and budget oversight of NRO activities.[*]

At the same time, DNRO James Plummer agreed to provide written Congressional Budget Justification Books (CBJB) to Congress, leading to detailed interactions, which included providing briefings, answering written questions, and supporting congressional staff visits to NRO facilities.

At the DoD, the Under Secretary of Defense (Policy), or USD (P), and the Assistant Secretary of Defense (C3I), or ASD/C3I, established staff elements to oversee the NRO. The National Security Council established a position focused on space, including DoD and NASA, as well as the NRO. Finally, President Carter directed that all of government implement "zero-based budgeting" that required a re-justification for every ongoing program or activity.

Near Real-Time Collection Systems. As near real-time imagery and signals intelligence satellite systems entered service, the NRO Staff initiated the development of an experimental van to demonstrate real-time Electronics Intelligence (Elint) downlinks directly to military field units. Also during this period, Congress established a program for the Tactical Exploitation of National Capabilities (TENCAP) that funded experiments leveraging NRO capabilities to support military operations. TENCAP offices were established in the NRO and in each of the military services. With the

---

[*]   USIB Committees, subordinate to the IC Staff, were responsible for establishing NRO collection requirements.

20

increasing number of NRO users involved in the requirements process, the NRO began publishing program-level details at a lower security classification, thus making the details of NRO systems more accessible to military users in particular.

Arms Control. Following the arms control successes of the Nixon administration, President Jimmy Carter wanted to reach a nuclear arms control agreement with the Soviet Union that reduced weapons held by both nations. After more than a half decade of the second round Strategic Arms Limitation Talks (SALT 2), Carter and General Secretary Brezhnev reached a treaty agreement in the summer of 1979. The treaty mandated additional nuclear arms verification requirements, causing President Carter to publicly acknowledge for the first time the existence of reconnaissance satellites. He did so to assure the American people that the terms of the treaty could be verified. However, the treaty was not put into effect because of the Soviet invasion of Afghanistan six months later and the presence of Soviet combat troops in Cuba.

1979 Iranian Revolution. The United States established intelligence collection sites in northern Iran to collect intelligence on Soviet missile test launches from their Tyuratam test facility in the southwest USSR. With the culmination of the Iranian revolution in the winter of 1979, the United States closed the sites in response to the anti-American policies of the new Islamic regime in Iran. Consequently, satellite collection gained increased priority to compensate for the lost ground-based collection capabilities abandoned in Iran.

Security. In the winter of 1977, Christopher Boyce, a TRW employee working on a classified program, was arrested for selling to the Soviets classified information on US intelligence collection capabilities. William Kampiles, a CIA clerk, obtained a manual on the NRO's KH-11 imagery satellite. He travelled to Greece and sold the highly classified document to the Soviets. Kampiles was arrested a year after Boyce. These two espionage cases revealed extensive technical details about NRO intelligence collection capabilities.

Launch Transition. The DCI's IC Staff initiated a series of requirements and systems studies to guide this transition which increased staff oversight and involvement and substantially increased the interface role of the NRO Staff. These external studies aimed at choosing what programs were to be funded and which would not, and they further exacerbated competition between program offices and their proposed solutions.

Difficulties in Developing the National Space Reconnaissance Architecture. Decisions whether to proceed with an advanced imaging capability and the appropriate mix of Elint satellites generated disagreements between the DCI and SECDEF that required Presidential decisions. Also, rivalry between the CIA (DCI Admiral Stansfield Turner) and DoD (particularly the Deputy USD (P), Admiral Daniel J. Murphy) impacted NRP architecture and funding decisions.

The Later Years—Reagan and Bush Administrations (1980-1990)

The Reagan defense build-up had many implications for the NRO and its Staff. New initiatives were funded, but there was an increase in the use of sub-compartments and "specials" to restrict the community of those with knowledge of the new capabilities. The Ballistic Missile Defense Initiative that eventually became the Strategic Defense Initiative (SDI) intersected on many levels with the NRO. The Soviet development and testing of anti-satellite weapons led fears that space was no longer a sanctuary. This resulted in new investments in the survivability and robustness of satellite systems. The continuity of government initiative also had many implications for the NRO, including integration with the national command and control architecture and a strong push for survivable and enduring reconnaissance. The creation of Air Force Space Command, and later Unified Space Command, created additional interactions to be managed by the Staff.

New treaties placed additional demands for treaty monitoring and verification. Technology advancements enabled one program to perform the missions that in past years required several programs, which fostered increased competition. The Defense Advanced Research Projects Agency (DARPA) and the military services explored new approaches to performing space intelligence tasks based on small satellite approaches that overlapped with the NRO's responsibilities, thus creating policy and internal political issues.

New Defense Organizations. DNRO Dr. Robert Hermann established the Defense Reconnaissance Support Program (DRSP) in 1981 as a budgetary vehicle for DoD to invest in NRO capabilities that improved support to military operations. The DRSP, although separate from the NRP and managed by the Defense Support Program Office (DSPO), was integrated with the NRP planning process.

The Strategic Defense Initiative Organization (SDIO) was created to explore technologies to defend against ballistic missiles. Initial efforts focused on space options and technologies underlying NRO programs and programs that could be used as anti-satellite weapons. A number of NRO-bred technologies were adopted by the SDIO. The initiative also created many security and policy issues impacting the NRO.

Launch Systems Recovery. As further detailed in Chapter 6, the Space Shuttle *Challenger* failure and subsequent space launch recovery impacted all aspects of the NRO, driving up costs and further increasing oversight. The DNRO, Secretary Pete Aldridge, led the recovery and initiated the Commercial Expendable Launch Vehicle (CELV) program for the nation. However, transitioning back to expendable launch systems necessitated extensive redesign of programs, as well as the development and production of new families of Expendable Launch Vehicles (ELVs).

Stand-up of United States Space Command and the Air Force Space Command. The NRO, having previously transitioned a number of officers to the Office of the Secretary of Defense and Air Staff policy and planning staffs, established working relationships associated with the formation of Air Force Space Command and subsequently a Unified Command for space, extending and defining national interests in space, while protecting NRO interests.

22

Chapter 5

ORGANIZATION OF THE NRO STAFF

Introduction

The NRO was created on 6 September 1961 with Dr. Joseph V. Charyk, the Under Secretary of the Air Force, and Dr. Richard Bissell, a senior CIA policy maker serving as co-Directors. During that time, Charyk was served by the staff of the Office of Missile and Satellite Systems (OMSS) [see Appendix 2], and the CIA staff served Bissell. In 1962 when Dr. Charyk became the single DNRO, the staff was reconstituted as the NRO Staff, with the unclassified designation of Office of the Secretary of the Air Force, Space Systems (SAFSS). Several, but not all, of the former OMSS staff transitioned to the new NRO Staff, including Brig Gen John L. Martin, the former Deputy Director of the OMSS Staff, who became the first Director of the NRO Staff.[26]

Although the roles and basic functions of the NRO Staff remained relatively stable over the course of its history, the *organization* of the elements which carried out those functions was modified by DNROs and Staff Directors in response to changing circumstances and their personal styles. In some cases, entire functions or missions such as the operational tasking of NRO satellites or management of airborne collectors were transferred from the Staff, precipitating substantial organizational changes to the Staff. In other instances, organizational changes were made in response to oversight changes, such as in the case of legislative liaison, or in response to changes in mission emphasis, such

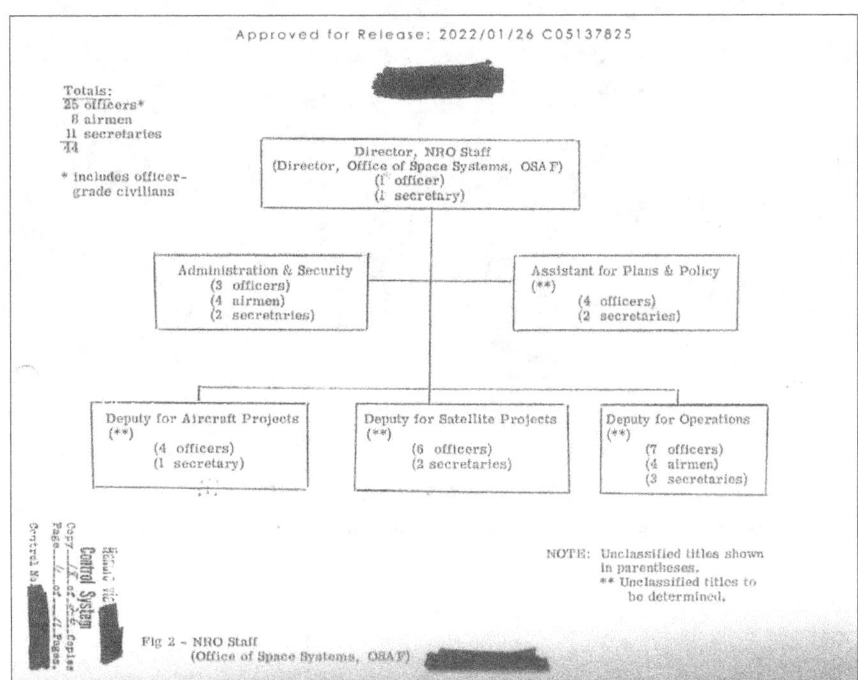

Fig 2 – NRO Staff
(Office of Space Systems, OSAF)

23

as support to military operations.

The Early Years (1962-74)

It was not until 23 July 1962, ten months after the creation of the National Reconnaissance Office that NRO Director Charyk established Program A (Air Force), Program B (CIA), and Program C (Navy). Soon thereafter Program D was established to manage CIA and Air Force airborne assets, such as the U-2 and SR-71 programs. Charyk established the NRO Staff with the same directive. The Staff's offices were located in the Pentagon, centered in Suite 4C-1000.

The **Assistant for Plans and Policy** was responsible for over-all assistance in establishing and maintaining NRO management procedures and the interface of such procedures with all Washington offices and agencies concerned. He was also responsible for handling State, United Nations, Disarmament, and DoD matters affecting the NRO or the NRP. He was assisted in this responsibility by a Deputy Assistant of Photo Plans and a Deputy Assistant of Sigint Plans. In order to assure that his responsibilities were discharged in critical appreciation of the state of NRP capabilities, limitations, and difficulties, the Assistant for Plans and Policy drew upon other members of the NRO Staff and members of the Program Directors' staffs for appropriate part-time assistance. Detailed studies of specific projects were assigned to the appropriate Program Director, as well as all studies for which contractual action was required.

1969 NRO STAFF LEADERSHIP

FROM L TO R: CAPT Geiger, Col Worthman, Brig Gen Berg, Col Allen, and Col Sweeney

24

The **Deputy for Aircraft Projects** assisted Program Directors in obtaining necessary support for all aircraft and drone projects of the NRP, and for keeping the DNRO currently informed on the status and capabilities of such projects. He was also responsible for coordination of US peripheral reconnaissance missions with aircraft and drone missions managed by the NRO.

The **Deputy for Satellite Projects** assisted Program Directors in obtaining necessary support for all satellite projects of the NRP, and for keeping the DNRO currently informed on the status and capabilities of such projects.

The **Deputy for Operations** was responsible for all satellite operations tasks assigned to the NRO Staff. He was responsible for coordination of US peripheral reconnaissance missions with satellite missions of the NRP. In addition, he was responsible for the NRO working interface with the USIB, which established overhead target requirements and priorities.

Dr. Charyk's NRO Staff of 1962 included several individuals that had served in the earlier Office of Missiles and Satellite Systems. Brig Gen Martin, previously Brig Gen Curtin's deputy in OMSS, was the first director of the NRO Staff. Lt Col Thomas Herron, Lt Col Robert A. Van Mater, Maj Henry C. Howard, and others transitioned to the newly formed NRO Staff.

Brig Gen Martin's 1962 NRO Staff organization had much more of a "staff" focus than the previous OMSS organization, judging from the position descriptions of the two organizations. One significant exception, however was mission planning, which was performed by the operations group within the NRO Staff. The group translated tasking requirements from the intelligence community into specific target decks, specifying desired targets to be covered, as well as desired on-orbit target program options. Otherwise, the role was that typical of a normal staff. With the exception of on-orbit planning discussed above, the program offices were responsible for carrying out the acquisition and execution phases for assigned programs.

Dr. Brockway McMillan
DNRO: 1 Mar 1963 - 1 Oct 1965

The first major modification to the Staff organization occurred in December 1963 when the second NRO Director, Brockway McMillan, established the Advanced Planning Office, reporting to the Staff Director.[27]

According to Perry's NRP history, "McMillan created an advanced planning office within the NRO Staff to evaluate and recommend matters involving future space research and development projects. His motivation was to counterbalance attractive CIA studies that might quickly be transformed into programs."[28]

This modification was significant in that it reflected a significant change in the Staff's authorities. However, a review of literature, as well as interviews conducted for this book, did not reveal any significant contributions of McMillan's Advanced Plans Group. It was dissolved when Dr. Alexander Flax became DNRO.

The Middle Years (1974-80)

As the stakeholder community grew larger, the Staff organization adjusted to these increased user needs. One growing need was to better support military operations. In 1974, Brig Gen Jack Kulpa, then serving as NRO Staff Director, established the Concepts and Applications Office to bring more focus on user needs, particularly those of the military services.[29] The branch initiated military support concepts, partnering with the military TENCAPs, and later with the DSPO in prioritizing and supporting defense-related initiatives. The branch functioned more as a line organization in conjunction with the Program A technology element in demonstrating the value of integrated Sigint/Imint tasking and exploitation, as well as the utility of delivering preprocessed signal data directly to the military user. This early demonstration of direct downlink of NRO data and integrated products set the stage for optimizing the intelligence and operational value of NRO products and demonstrated that NRO systems could be operationally relevant.

The Concepts and Applications Office directly supported the newly formed NRO Tactical Exploitation of National Capabilities and Applications Program (NRO TENCAP), led by COL Ronald Lemanski (USA) who reported directly to the DNRO. This DSPO/TENCAP/ NRO Staff partnership extended Brig Gen Kulpa's vision of focusing on support to military operations, making NRO national systems relevant to the military operator, as was ultimately and conclusively demonstrated during the first Gulf War.

Dr. Hans M. Mark
DNRO: 3 Aug 1977 - 8 Oct 1979

In November 1977, Dr. Hans Mark proposed at his second Program Directors meeting a new "organizational framework" for the NRO Staff. He suggested three staff elements: Liaison and Administration, Programs and Budget, and Concepts and Applications. After four months of staffing with his management team, Mark signed a memorandum to 39 Washington seniors announcing his newly organized NRO Staff, effective 1 April 1978.[30] His new construct included three major staff elements as depicted below:

The **Directorate of Liaison and Administration,** led by Col Nate Lindsay, served as the Staff interface on policy and administration matters between the NRO and other members of the Executive Department (e.g., NASA, NSC, and the Arms Control and Disarmament Agency), provided administrative support for the NRO headquarters, and assisted the DNRO with security policy, procedures, and practices. The Directorate oversaw the management of all secure communications for the NRP. The Directorate also served as the focal point for the NRO on all public information and was further divided into six elements: Staff & Policy Interface, Security Policy, Operational Policy, Administrative Support, Personnel, and Communications Management.

The **Directorate of Programs and Budget,** led by Lt Col Dave "Bud" Doyle, assisted the DNRO in formulating fiscal guidance to the program offices, developing the NRP budget, and implementing the fiscal program of the NRP. They maintained interface with the Congress and with programming and budgeting elements of the Executive Department. The Directorate was subdivided into four elements: Programs and Budget, Financial Administration, Congressional Liaison, and Logistics and Procurement.

The **Directorate of Systems and Technology,** led by Tom Appleberry, functioned as the technical monitor for programs and as the consultant on program status to NRO customers as well as NRO program offices. The staff element also provided representation to DCI committees and other technical committee functions. The S&T Directorate was further divided into two elements: Satellite Programs and Research & Analysis.

Concurrently, Dr. Mark established the NRO TENCAP office, reporting to the DNRO, and headed by COL Ronald Lemanski, USA.

26

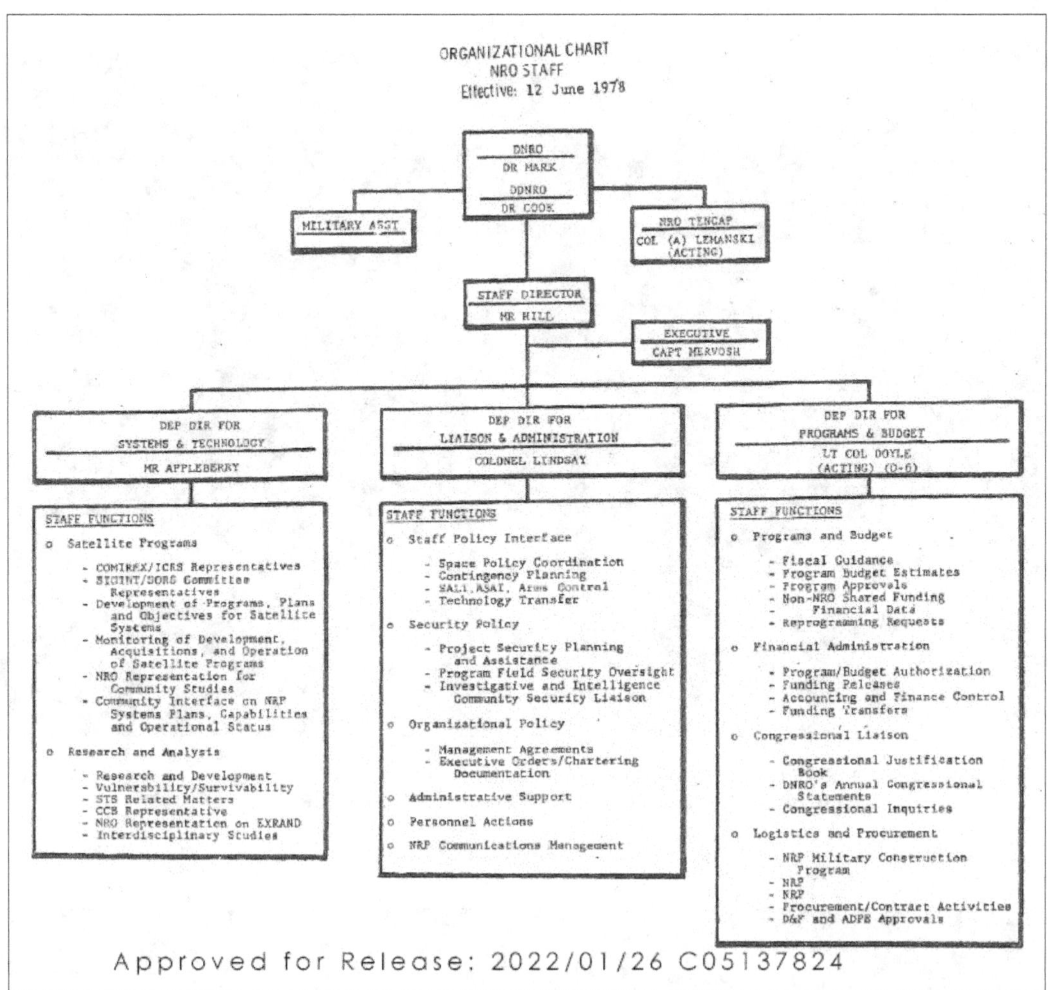

Shortly after announcing the Staff reorganization, Hans Mark announced the appointment of Mr. Jimmie Hill as the Director of the NRO Staff and distributed an organizational chart for the new organization. It should be noted that the updated organization did not include an operations function, as the imagery related functions of the Satellite Operations Center (SOC) had been transferred to California the previous year, and the Sigint related functions had been transferred to the NRO/NSA jointly-manned Overhead Collection Management Center (OCMC) in Ft. Meade.[31]

27

BACK ROW: COL Ronald Lemanski (USA), Col Jim Fitzgibbon, Lt Col Phil Bracher, Lt Col Don Hard, Capt Jim Boyle
FRONT ROW: Col Joe Eash, Mr. Jimmie Hill, Col George Mushalko. **PHOTO:** Early 1981

BACK ROW: Col Charlie Anderson, Chief of Staff, Col Bill Savage, Plans, CAPT Jim Barnet (USN), Budget, COL Charles Solohub (USA), Richard Taylor, NSA Rep, Senior Sigint PEM, Lt Col Phil Pounds, Security, Capt Kevin McLaughlin, Launch
FRONT ROW: Col John Graves, Communications, Mr. John Sharrard, Senior Imint PEM, Brig Gen Don Walker, Staff Director, Col Hal Gordon, Policy, Col Jim Kindle **PHOTO:** 1989-90

The Later Years (1980-90)

For the years following the 1978 Staff reorganization, a review of a number of various papers such as organization charts and phone listings revealed only minor changes to the Staff's organizational structure.

Beginning in 1984, there were a number of changes to the Staff organization. For example, "Liaison and Security" was changed to "Policy and Security," with "Personnel" reporting to the Staff Executive, and "Congressional Matters" reporting directly to the Staff Director, rather than to the Budget Director, a further strengthening of the Legislative Liaison function. "Long Range Plans" was added as a third sub-element of Systems and Technology. Finally, in June 1989, "Plans & Analysis" replaced "Plans and Studies." This 15-person staff element, led initially by Lt Col Phil Datema, who was replaced by Col Bill Savage, reported directly to the Staff Director. The addition of this NRO Staff element was significant in that it was a precursor for a much more robust, independent Plans and Analysis group, reporting directly to the Director of the NRO.

The bottom left photograph captures the last 4C-1000 NRO Staff leadership team, taken in late 1989 or early 1990.

Chapter 6

ROLES AND FUNCTIONS OF THE NRO STAFF

As noted previously, the NRO Staff, as created by Dr. Charyk in September 1962, was a small, highly streamlined staff organization with talented and empowered officers supporting the DNRO. This chapter will describe the roles and functions of the NRO Staff.

Roles of the Staff

With the exception of Satellite Operations, the roles performed by the NRO Staff were stable throughout its existence. However, the environment in which it performed these roles did change in terms of stakeholders, oversight, and technology.

The 4C-1000 Staff performed the following roles:

- Develop, promote, and defend an *integrated* National Reconnaissance Program
- Facilitate and support the NRO line organizations
- Represent NRO interests with stakeholders
- Support the NRO decision processes
- Provide specialized security, communications, and personnel processes
- Operational level command and control (1962–1974)

Interestingly, this statement of the *roles* of the NRO Staff did not change substantially from the formulation of the Staff in 1962 until early 1990, when the NRO Staff as we knew it, small and streamlined, centrally located in the Pentagon with a Staff Director reporting to the NRO Director, began to be absorbed into a much larger restructured NRO organization. Also, during this period there was reasonably few changes in the *functions* performed by the Staff in the execution of its role. The *organizational* changes to the Staff were more numerous, as reflected by changes in organizational designations and actual organizational charts, and of course the people or individuals assigned to the Staff, who generally rotated every two to three years.

The following chart compares the basic *roles* of the original Staff in 1962, as specifically defined by Dr. Charyk in 1962[32] compared to an *interpreted* description of the Staff's roles in 1990. This illustrates the assertion that the role and basic functions of the Staff changed little over the 28-year course of the Staff.

31

1962[33]	**1990**[34]

Brig Gen John Martin –First NRO Staff Director	Brig Gen Don Walker —Last NRO Staff Director

PROJECT OVERSIGHT	
Assist the DNRO to maintain current knowledge of the status of each project of the NRP.	Unchanged.

Comment: *In 1990 the number of programs grew, yet the role of the Staff technical and budget monitors remained the same, focusing on individual programs and maintaining technical and financial status for the DNRO.*

EXECUTIVE DECISION SUPPORT	
Assist the Program Directors by accomplishing all project matters which require action above the Program Director's level in Washington.	Unchanged.

Comment: *Consistent with Jimmie Hill's view that the Staff's role was to assist, rather than challenge the program offices.*

STAKEHOLDER RELATIONSHIP MANAGEMENT	
Establish and maintain the NRO interface with the USIB and with the principal users of NRP results.	Establish and maintain the NRO interface with Congress, the IC Staff, and the principal users of NRP results, including DoD and Service Staffs.

Comment: *Although the oversight body and user community changed organizationally, the basic function remained the same. There was increased interface with DoD and Service Staffs with key participation in studies from C3I, Air Staff, and Navy.*

OPERATIONS	
Carry out the operational responsibilities described as functions of the NRO Staff, including satellite mission planning from the point of view of selection of targets and target options, and exercise of all on-orbit target options.	Operational responsibilities transitioned from the Staff to community managed functions at Ft. Meade (SIGINT) (IMINT).

Comment: *The Satellite Operation Center which previously carried out operational responsibilities for NRO Systems was disbanded in 1978. Although Air Force members of the OCMC reported administratively through the Staff Director, the staff had no operational responsibilities.*

RECONNAISSANCE COORDINATION	
Coordinate all peripheral reconnaissance activities of the U. S. with the missions of the NRP.	No staff responsibility.

Comment: *The NRO Staff did not engage in reconnaissance coordination activities outside of the NRO contrary to expectations in 1962. By 1990, the total breadth of US reconnaissance activities had greatly expanded.*

32

1962[33]	1990[34]
PARENT ORGANIZATION LIAISON	
Keep designated personnel in each Service and specified Agency completely informed on the content and status of the NRP in order that they may take action necessary to prepare for adequate exploitation of the collected intelligence products.	Unchanged.
Comment: *The 1990 NRO Staff worked closely with the intelligence and mapping organizations, many of which were represented on the NRO Staff.*	
STUDIES	
Conduct studies of the overall NRP to determine the most reasonable combination of projects and number of missions that should be planned to meet the total requirements and priorities established by USIB.	*The extent to which the NRO Staff conducted studies and performed analysis on the optimal "combination of projects and number of missions" was era dependent. By 1990 the growth of community requirements and the complexity of NRO systems and architectures outgrew the Staff's capability for analytic study support. This led to the formation of Plans & Analysis in 1990, a robust, independent analytical element reporting directly to the DNRO.*
OUTSIDE REQUIREMENTS MANAGEMENT	
Monitor and take all necessary staff action to handle State Department, UN, DoD, JCS, and Congressional matters which affect the NRO or NRP.	Unchanged.
STREAMLINE MANAGEMENT PRACTICES	
Assist the DNRO in establishing and maintaining effective streamlined management procedures appropriate to the mission of the NRO and consistent with the security considerations which apply.	Unchanged.
Comment: *Although the size of the NRO Staff grew and the NRO as a whole saw orders-of-magnitude increases in growth, much of the expansion can be attributed to comparable increases in mission growth, as well as additional layers of community and Congressional oversight.*	
DNRO STAFFING SUPPORT	
Provide staff support to the DNRO for any matter required in connection with his duties, including preparation of reports, illustrations, and briefings covering any aspect of the NRP.	Unchanged.
INTERNAL POLICY DEVELOPMENT	
Not addressed.	Develop NRO policy as relates to internal NRO practices, as well as in its interactions with the larger national space, intelligence, and operational communities.
SECURITY	
Not addressed.	Develop and execute NRO security policies and practices.
Comment: *The growing complexity of users, overlapping of mission domains, and growing organizational interdependencies over time required increased focus in Staff policy and security functions. Also, as the systems became more "real-time" useful to the military, the service and DoD interfaces grew. The implications of the formation of the DRSP and the cancelation of the SR-71 are examples.*	

33

Functions of NRO Staff

The NRO Staff was organized with functional leads reporting to the Staff Director. The titles of the Staff organization were realigned over time, with functional elements occasionally moving from one sub-element to another with few exceptions.

It should also be noted that within the Staff, organizational lines and hence functional responsibilities were not rigidly followed. Often the most qualified Staff member was assigned a task, regardless of the individual's "home room." One of the objectives of this section is to address the functions, rather than the organizational entity, which were covered in the preceding chapter.

Security

What led President Eisenhower to require such a high magnitude of secrecy and security in his design of a national overhead reconnaissance program? The answer may be found in the experiences that shaped his thinking about security and his understanding of "Must-know." He knew from his wartime experience the value of reliable intelligence required for strategic decisions. That confidence increased when the intelligence target did not know the capabilities of the collection effort used against it. The National Reconnaissance Program and the office that managed that program would be covert, hidden from all those without a "Must-know." The NRP would include aircraft overflight with the existing security of the early 1960s.

Execution Authorities

The NRO security staff's responsibilities and day-to-day activities fulfilled the security-related terms of an NRO agreement between the DCI and the SECDEF in May 1962.[35] While the implementation agreement, signed by the Director of Central Intelligence and the Deputy Secretary of Defense, assigned operational responsibility and control of the NRP to the SECDEF, NRP security responsibility was retained by the DCI, consistent with his statutory security authorities as Director of the CIA. Since the NRO was a DoD organization, DCI/CIA execution of security responsibilities for the NRP required the assignment of a CIA Office of Security officer to the NRO Staff to represent and manage that responsibility for the NRP. Administrative supervision of the CIA Office of Security representative (a GS-15 position) was jointly managed by the NRO Deputy Director and the Director of the CIA Office of Security. An Air Force officer was assigned to the office as deputy to the CIA assignee. Both officers executed the assigned CIA and DoD security authorities for the NRP as the security staff Component of the NRO Staff. The CIA officer was assigned CIA statutory "Original Classification Authority" and Compartmented Security authorities from the DCI.

This unique arrangement enabled the NRO Security Office to create and integrate DoD and CIA statutory security authorities and develop policies as required for the statutory DoD "Original Classification Authority," as well as employ the DCI's authorities as deputy to the CIA officer protecting the NRO and NRP. In addition, the security staff represented and executed the responsibilities for NRP security within the NRO, DoD, and across the government without regard to the officers' organization of origin. Initially the office was comprised of only these two officers and a secretary. The security staff's mission provided sufficient secrecy for the NRP to ensure its intelligence mission was successful.

Key Responsibilities and Organizational Interfaces

Achievement of NRO/NRP secrecy required extensive and regular liaison with both operational and security staffs from most Executive Branch departments and agencies, including the National Security Council staff for NRP Sources and Methods. These Sources and Methods reviews of other Departments' and Agencies' internal documents, plans, and public releases was a daily routine. For

34

example, CIA National Intelligence Estimates were sent to the security staff in the 1960s and 70s for an NRP Sources and Methods exposure review. A frequent performance requirement involved coordination and containment of imminent potential public exposures of the NRO or NRP related information throughout the Executive Branch.

General monitoring and oversight of the NRO enterprise and its operations required a broad and detailed knowledge of NRO and NRP operations. A working knowledge of details of its activities, interfaces, and operations was essential to execution of the daily activities. The security staff conducted regular visits to Satellite Program Offices, operational facilities, and industrial facilities. These often occurred at the request of program office security staffs and always in coordination with them. These visits included comprehensive and detailed reviews and audits of cover, concealment, and other secrecy practices and procedures at all prime and sub-contractor facilities. Results of these reviews were reported to the program offices' security staff for their action.

Byeman Control System

Information revealing the existence and details of the NRO and the NRP, as well as technical details about NRO systems, were classified and controlled within the Byeman security control system. Certain organizational information and intelligence collected by the NRP were controlled in the Talent-Keyhole and other compartments. As a result, most of the security staff's efforts were related to the Byeman security policies. However, the nature of covert overhead reconnaissance secrecy required a very active engagement in the establishment and monitoring of IC sources and methods protection policies, practices, and procedures. The two security staff officers actively supported IC committees relevant to NRO and related sources and methods protection. The NRO authorities to protect the secrecy of NRO operations were substantial and recognized by the Congressional intelligence committees. This Congressional support was particularly significant since the community committees were responsible for the Talent-Keyhole sub-compartments, which enabled intelligence analysts, for example, to train on future systems without requiring Byeman access.

Features of the Byeman security system included:

- Minimizing the number of accessed personnel with knowledge of critical secrets.

- Compartmenting all aspects of NRO activities so that the fewest possible number of individuals were knowledgeable of the details of any single program.

- Requiring comprehensive background investigations (initial and periodic reinvestigations) and subsequent counter-intelligence polygraphs.

- Minimizing disclosed technical information required to achieve operational or interface needs.

- Requiring third-party introductions to verify mutual security credentials.

- Requiring an indoctrination briefing tailored to the functions of the engineer, scientist, administrative worker, etc. Each person *owned* the security of his or her respective function.[36]

> "The office will consist of carefully selected personnel of the highest qualifications, and will be confined to the minimum number required to accomplish the task under the conditions which apply."
>
> — Joseph Charyk,
> July 1962

The NRO security staff designed and supported a wide array of cover arrangements, as required to support or sustain the secrecy of NRO operations and essential interfaces, often requiring extensive and direct security staff interaction in DoD and other Executive Branch departments and agencies.

Over the years, the need for security drove, enabled, and protected every element of the NRO at every level. The volume of information flowing through the security staff for classification, compartmentation, and accuracy verification from other components of the government was extremely high. Eventually, the security staff produced compartmentation and classification guides for external departments and agencies to assist in reducing the dependency on the NRO Staff for the increasing volume caused by the growth of NRP programs and operations. The security staff responsibilities that extended into other departments and agencies created a trusted collaborative web of relationships across the Executive Branch that enabled the flow of multi-level information, while protecting sensitive NRP operations and programmatic information.

During the 28-year span of the NRO Staff, a total of only five rotating Air Force officers were assigned to the security staff, four of which typically rotated between the Staff and Program A.[37] With few exceptions, rotation of the CIA officers was more frequent. Nevertheless, service by this very small cadre, which generally never exceeded one Air Force officer and one CIA senior civilian at a time, was a major factor in the continuity and success of NRO secrecy for nearly three decades.

Personnel

The NRO Staff's personnel management section provided the interface between the other Staff elements and the service and agency personnel systems in the selection and retention of Staff personnel, as well as managing other personnel actions which included training, performance evaluation, and in some cases relocation. Each service and agency had a different process for selecting, assigning, and retaining people allocated to NRO duty. The Air Force developed a special assignment section within the Air Force Personnel Center specifically to manage NRO assignments. It serviced both the Staff and Program A and had the authority to waive many standard personnel management policies and regulations. The Army and Navy had no similar process, as their numbers were much smaller. Typically, assignments for both services were handled on a case-by-case basis. Of note, even within the Navy's Program C, there were few uniformed Navy personnel, as most of the program management and development work was accomplished by the Naval Research Laboratory's civilian workforce.

The CIA had special hiring authorities and assigned people to the NRO and Program B on a case-by-case basis, with assignees largely staying within the agency's Office of Development and Engineering (OD&E) for their entire careers. Relatively few CIA officers served tours on the NRO Staff, and these were handled on a case-by-case basis. The NRO was unusual in that people were selected without undue concern for their job specialty codes. For example, a Program Element Monitor position might be filled with an engineer, a program manager, an intelligence specialist, or a pilot, and the job specialty of an incumbent might be different from their replacement in the same NRO Staff position.

Air Force Personnel Management

Selection of the Staff Director was, typically, an Air Force Brigadier General, selected by the DNRO and often subsequently assigned to be the Director of Program A. Other key positions reporting directly to the Staff Director were typically selected through collaboration between the Staff Director and program office directors, in some cases also involving the Director or Deputy Director of the NRO. At lower levels, Staff appointments were made with the approval of the Staff Director, in many cases the result of a very active vetting process at lower levels.

In the case of those appointments representing the operations and intelligence communities, individuals were nominated by seniors in their home offices and vetted in a similar manner as those coming from NRO program offices. This entire selection process was managed by the NRO Staff personnel group. With respect to Air Force assignments, which represented the majority of the Staff positions, the Staff personnel group worked closely with the "Green Door" at the Air Force Military Personnel Center (AFMPC) at Randolph Air Force Base (AFB), Texas to facilitate the assignment action. It should be noted that the Green Door process was an informal designation of the Air Force Special Assignments group activities at AFMPC. Interaction between AFMPC and NRO elements was facilitated by secure phones and a Secure Compartmented Information Facility (SCIF) at AFMPC. This alliance between AFMPC and the NRO Staff also applied to Air Force staff assigned to Program A, with the NRO Staff providing a coordinated response to AFMPC.

The NRO Staff personnel group was able to leverage this process for Air Force assignments, in most cases interacting directly with the Special Assignments Group, and including an input from Program A for a consolidated NRO response.

Just as important as selecting the right personnel for Air Force positions in the NRO was retaining those individuals, many of whom spent the majority of their careers in the NRO. The process for identifying those who should be retained was the Personnel Control List (PCL), which was reviewed and updated on an annual basis. The Air Force PCL listed all of the NRO officers with currently approved rotation dates. The Staff Director had the discretion to extend each officer's rotation date with the understanding that the individual would be protected from reassignment by the Air Force's Special Assignments Group. Since the Program A input was integrated into the NRO's Air Force PCL, managed by the Staff Director, the NRO had the ability to retain Air Force officers within the NRO for the better part of an individual's career, helping to maintain an NRO space cadre of highly experienced officers, to the point that it was not uncommon for senior Air Force officers to aspire to Colonel, but then elect to stay in position in the NRO, rather than compete for Brigadier General if it meant leaving the NRO.[38]

The Air Force Communications Service (AFCS), which later became the Air Force Communications Command, provided communications support at NRO facilities world-wide, and also prioritized the selection and retention of NRO communicators. The senior communicator at NRO operational locations was "dual-hatted," reporting through NRO as well as AFCS channels, and in this role actively engaged in the NRO/AFCS assignment process.[39]

The Staff personnel group is also credited for creating a career track in the mid-1960s for young Air Force officers, colloquially referred to as "Wizards." In a collaborative effort with the Special Assignments Group, the Air Force Institute of Technology (AFIT), the Rochester Institute of Technology (RIT), and Eastman Kodak, officers would graduate from RIT with a Master's degree in Photographic Science, followed by a one-year assignment with Eastman Kodak, under sponsorship of the AFIT's Education With Industry (EWI) program. Officers were then typically assigned to Program A program offices, or in some instances, the NRO Staff technology group.[40]

37

CIA Personnel Management

The Program B director selected and directly hired many of his program's office staff. The Agency had special hiring authorities that allowed the direct hire of technical experts at relatively senior levels and at high pay grades. The Staff's interface for personnel management of CIA people was the CIA Office of Development and Engineering personnel group, which among other things managed the OD&E Personnel Assignment Group (PAG). The PAG was typically chaired by the director or deputy director of OD&E with representation by each of the directors/deputies who would map out assignment actions for each of the OD&E officers, including those assigned to the NRO Staff. Assignment actions were similarly vetted with the NRO Staff Director, and in some cases, the DNRO.

Navy Personnel Management

The Navy personnel system did not have such a specialized assignment office. Instead, the positions were coded for the skills required, and the institutional navy assignment system provided regular support. For Program C operation, positions were allocated to the Naval Security Group and staffed from within that Command. For systems development, the Navy relied on a large component of Navy civilian workers who stayed in place for their careers. The active duty management came from within the Program C engineering staff, with senior managers personally selected by the Program C Director, a Navy Admiral or Captain, similar to the final selection process for senior officers in Programs A and B.

Satellite Operations

The NRO's role in satellite operations was a contentious issue when the NRO was formed. A CIA clandestine Operations Center existed in Palo Alto, California that had its origins in the planning and tasking of U-2 overflight missions, and it had become the planning center for early Corona missions. Director Charyk argued successfully to have the satellite portion of that Ops Center, along with experienced Corona operations personnel, realigned under him as the DNRO and to have the activity relocated to the Pentagon. This outcome was of immediate benefit to the objective of a consolidated National Reconnaissance Program.[41]

> *The SOC was located in the basement of the Pentagon (Room BD944), leading to its informal designation, "The Mushroom Factory."*

The Satellite Operations Center was aligned as an NRO Staff element in 1962. The Satellite Ops functions were not traditional Staff functions; but at the time, Programs A, B, and C were semi-autonomous entities, and the only organization that was wholly responsive to the DNRO was what became the NRO Staff that same year. The SOC was located in the basement of the Pentagon (Room BD944), leading to its informal designation, "The Mushroom Factory."

Under Dr. Charyk's direction, the NRO Staff was responsible for detailed mission planning, including specifying desired targets to be covered and approval of the actual mission target options which were programmed into each flight vehicle. The Staff made all on-orbit selections between target coverage options based on weather and/or intelligence factors. They also coordinated satellite operations with other collection activities, such as the Joint Chiefs of Staff (JCS)-managed Peacetime Aerial Reconnaissance Program (PARPRO).

38

Of note, the CIA proposed that the Ops Center be transferred back to CIA. Disagreeing, Director McMillan underscored the importance of the NRO maintaining responsibility for mission planning and tasking functions stating, "I am convinced that if the Op Center is removed from the NRO, the NRO will be destroyed and the DoD will experience interminable difficulties in getting its requirements recognized."[42]

The NRO Staff Deputy Director for Operations, who reported to the Staff Director, headed the SOC. In addition to its operations role, SOC personnel represented the NRO to the USIB and its committees, whose functions included both short-term collection priorities and future system requirements. As the USIB interface, the SOC also represented the NRO in supporting development of community requirements for new system capabilities (including participation on system trade studies) and coordinating with other Staff elements and program offices.

Within the SOC there was an Imagery branch, a Sigint branch, a Logistics branch, a weather liaison, and other operations support functions. The operations role evolved over time as computer tools were introduced, systems got more capable and complex, and requirements grew in scope and detail. The staff provided technical assistance and worked with the requirements committees to define specific collection requirements and then developed tasking documents that were provided to mission ground stations, where they were converted into satellite commands and loaded into the systems.

The Logistics Branch maintained a depot to support satellite operations and also managed and coordinated transportation requirements associated with moving satellites and components among factories and launch pads, or as was required. The branch had the authority to exercise the highest national security priority, Brickbat 1, to meet program needs.

A weather liaison element from the Air Force Weather Service supported imagery mission planning and also provided space weather support, as required. Similarly, a representative from the Defense Mapping Agency was assigned to support operations planning.

The NRO jealously guarded their responsibilities for tasking systems (translating community priorities into specific mission tasking). There was always tension between the roles of the NRO (tasking) and the NSA (providing specific Sigint technical guidance). NRO Detachment Ft. Meade (NDF) was established in 1976 to help address these tensions and also to better deal with systems that were becoming timelier and more interactive. At that time, the Sigint branch was split, with four people staying in the Pentagon and four moving to Ft. Meade. The NDF was collocated with the Poppy Ops Center (which reported to NRO Program C and served a satellite control facility-type function for the Poppy Elint satellite system) and with an NSA consolidated center that included representatives from several different NSA directorates. While the elements were collocated in the same room, they were not combined or integrated, and each had a reporting chain back to their parent organization. The NRO Detachment Commander reported to the Sigint Branch Chief at the Pentagon, who in turn worked for the NRO Staff Deputy Director for Operations.

Staffing of the Ops Center organization was different from the other NRO Staff elements, in that assigned personnel were, for the most part, not drawn from nor returned to Programs A, B, or C. The Imagery branch members were largely government civilian employees (mostly retired military pilots) who made their second career in the SOC. Imagery personnel had very little turnover. The Sigint branch was different in that it included primarily active duty combat arms officers. There were Navy surface warfare officers, Air Force pilots and Sigint specialists, Army artillery and infantry officers, and government civilians from outside the NRO. In Sigint, there was a fair amount of turnover, with most of those leaving for assignments outside the NRO. Primarily, Air Force logistics officers staffed the Logistics branch, and the weather and other liaison positions were staffed with subject matter experts.

39

By the mid-1970s, the advent of more timely and interactive satellite systems, coupled with more capable computerized requirements systems, was stressing the ability of the NRO Satellite Ops Center to do its job. In 1977, the NRO moved the Hexagon mission planning and tasking functions from the SOC to the Satellite Control Facility in Sunnyvale, CA and combined them with the command generation function. In 1978, the NRO disestablished the SOC. The imaging tasking functions of the community and NRO were consolidated at the imagery system site; the Sigint functions were consolidated at Ft. Meade and integrated with the NSA technical guidance functions to create the jointly-staffed Overhead Collection Management Center. The liaison interfaces that had been aligned to the SOC were realigned, with Logistics going to Program A and weather liaison along with a few remaining ops staff personnel remaining on the NRO Staff, but transferring to what was then Programs & Budget.

With the demise of the SOC, the NRO interface to the USIB committees and the newly created Intelligence Community Staff was divided. Systems and Technology became responsible for new system requirements and future system studies, while Liaison and Administration became responsible for related policy coordination. The OCMC became a joint organization, but the NRO personnel assigned to that organization continued to be rated by the NRO Staff Director, even though the OCMC functions were never integrated into the Staff.

Policy

The NRO Staff included a policy function focused on coordinating internal and external policy issues that had implications for the NRO and with protecting the organization's interests. The scope of policies this small team worked on was extensive.

KEY POLICY FUNCTIONS

- Reviewing and contributing to the development of high-level policy documents such as Presidential Directives, Executive Orders, and decision memoranda to ensure NRO interests were protected.

- Protecting the authorities, responsibilities, and accountabilities assigned to the NRO by policy and charter. This included developing NRO internal policies, and negotiation of management agreements (or memorandums of agreement) with other government departments or agencies.

- Representing the DNRO in high-level policy forums involving space or arms control policies, treaties, and legal or legislative actions that had ramifications for the NRO.

- Providing staff support for reviewing technology transfer requests, Freedom of Information requests, contingency planning, and other government deliberations and decisions that had ramifications for NRO equities.

- Developing, in coordination with the security function,* policies that governed compartmentation and personnel access control to protect security and to enable and maintain the streamlined organization and management structure.

---

* The security function of the NRO Staff was at times combined with the policy function; otherwise it reported separately to the Staff Director. Security had a broad mandate for developing, executing, and overseeing security policy. The policy element coordinated policy development but was not responsible for its execution. Regardless, the policy team was, in all cases, involved in security policy issues of sufficient magnitude to concern the DNRO.

40

The number of policy issues impacting NRO equities increased over time as the utility of space systems increased, the community of users expanded, and budgets grew, resulting in an increased industrial base and more and broader oversight. Security breaches occurred creating legal and security challenges, as technologies underpinning NRO systems proliferated to other countries and to private commercial enterprises.

Due to the streamlined nature of the NRO Staff, the policy team was small, with relatively junior officers, generally never exceeding five officers total. Because of security constraints that limited access, their counterparts in other organizations were often higher ranking or otherwise more senior. There was very little intermediate management in the NRO Staff, so junior policy officers often worked directly with the Staff Director or the DDNRO. By the late 1970s, the DNRO often worked directly with the policy action officers to decide on policy objectives. He largely trusted them to use their judgment and exercise initiative in working policy issues to achieve the desired objectives.

By the late 1970s, DoD and National Space Policy activity had expanded to include a rapidly expanding array of stakeholders—civil government, foreign, and private sector interests that previously had no need-to-know about the NRO or details of its programs. To address these issues, a new three-person office was established within the Air Force Secretariat (Office of Space Policy, SAF/SX). Dr. Charlie Cook moved from his position as DDNRO to lead the office that was staffed by officers with significant prior NRO experience, including Col Seb Coglitore, Lt Col Jim Beale and Lt Col Ted Mervosh. The office worked closely with the NRO Staff's policy staff, as well as with the broader Air Force, and reported to the DNRO in his Air Force capacity. Initially the office dealt largely with NASA, negotiating Memorandums of Agreement (MOAs) on shuttle and other shared infrastructure agreements, including costs and cost reimbursement rates. It also served as the interface for issues involving, foreign space, the United Nations, and the emerging commercial space activities. It also served as a cut-out in representing NRO as well as Air Force interests with the White House Economic Council, the US Trade Representative, the Department of Transportation, and the Department of Commerce/National Oceanic and Atmospheric Administration.

Finally, the Staff policy function served as Staff lead for various external and expert panel studies or advisory groups that supported the DNRO on critical institutional decisions.

The Early Years (1962-74). Many of the policy issues of the early NRO dealt with establishing the roles, responsibilities, and authorities of the DNRO. During the years when Dr. Charyk and Dr. McMillan served as DNRO, policy issues were often worked in principals' meetings and in exchanges of letters. Key players were the senior CIA and DoD leadership, with many decisions going to the Deputy Secretary of Defense for resolution. The NRO Staff supported the DNRO in these negotiations and decision processes.

Some of the major activities supported by the policy staff, led by Col Paul Worthman, included development of the NRO charter documents in 1963 and 1965, interaction with the President's Foreign Intelligence Advisory Board regarding both oversight and organizational studies, and development of contingency plans for serious security disclosures or events that might cause an international incident. The policy staff was a key player in the negotiations between the NRO and the Air Force regarding the Manned Orbiting Laboratory program, and were essential in the documentation of the roles of the Strategic Air Command and the NRO for funding and operation of reconnaissance vehicles including the U-2, A-12, and SR-71 aircraft programs, as well as the D-21 drone program.[43]

By the time Dr. Flax became the DNRO in 1965, the early organizational issues were largely resolved. The NRO Executive Committee was formed as the decision authority for resolving conflicts and providing program and budget oversight. The policy staff supported the DNRO's participation in EXCOM meetings and drafted the meeting minutes.

Hexagon (KH-9) satellite pre-launch - 15 June 1971

During this time, technologies were advancing and new satellite programs provided increased capability to support a wider range of user needs. The policy staff primarily provided background information and staff support for the DNRO's external meetings, and drafted memos to prepare him on the key meeting issues.

Some of the external policy issues effecting NRO equities during the later years of the Johnson and Nixon Administrations that the policy staff was involved with included the Outer Space Treaty, which bans the stationing of weapons of mass destruction (WMD) in outer space, prohibits military activities on celestial bodies, and details legally binding rules governing the peaceful exploration and use of space; the Nuclear non-Proliferation Treaty, designed to restrict the spread of nuclear weapons beyond those countries that already had such weapons; and the SALT 1 interim agreement and Anti-Ballistic Missile treaty, which was the first agreement that referred to "National Technical Means of Verification" and the first public acknowledgement of the "fact of" satellite reconnaissance as a treaty verification tool.

The policy staff was utilized for President Johnson's public disclosure of the existence of the SR-71 program, the eventual cancellation of the A-12 and D-21 airborne reconnaissance programs, and the closure of NRO's Program D and the transfer of personnel and technologies to the Air Force.

Clockwise from Left: SR-71, A-12 and D-21B Drone on the wing of a B-52.

43

The Middle Years (1974-80). Several events during the mid- to late 1970s had a profound impact on the NRO policy function — dramatically increasing the role, engagement, and influence of the NRO policy staff on development of national security and intelligence community management policies. These events included an increase in the Soviet threat to national security space systems; Congressional concerns regarding the management and oversight of the Intelligence Community, highlighted by the Church/Pike Committee hearings and the subsequent reforms; the introduction of near real-time systems, coupled with a growing appreciation of the increasing capabilities of space systems to support military operations; and the development of the Space Shuttle and the expansion of its role as a critical launch system for NRO, as well as other DoD payloads.

These developments underscored the need for more comprehensive national-level direction from the White House and Congress. Accordingly, during this five-year period, there were a heretofore unprecedented number of space-related policies and directives issued. The Staff was deeply involved in reviewing each of these documents and, in many cases, provided language that was adopted for policies that were especially relevant to the NRO interest and equities.[*]

This period was a very active time in terms of the impact of national and DoD policy on the NRO, and the three young officers performing the NRO Staff policy functions were Lt Col Tom Moorman and Majors Jimmey Morrell and Dave Messner (often referred to as the 3-M's). They interfaced extensively with OSD, IC, Congressional, and White House staff elements, as well as those of the military departments. They explained the implications of various policy options and helped draft and coordinate policy documents, while advocating for and protecting NRO management and security equities. They also interfaced with NRO program offices and other Staff elements to help manage changes.

These policy deliberations/decisions drove major changes in oversight and priorities for the NRO. The recognition that space was not a sanctuary resulted in significant new investments in satellite survivability to respond to the increasing Soviet anti-satellite threat. The EXCOM was replaced by much more inclusive oversight processes, including both Congressional and Departmental staff involvement. The increased priority and funding for support to military operations included new funding mechanisms, as well as increases in the cleared requirements and size of the user community. Acknowledgement of the fact of overhead reconnaissance for treaty verification (National Technical Means of Verification) resulted in substantially increased attention, which strained security measures and resources.

The Later Years (1980-90). This period saw the policy team dealing with a technology–driven expansion in the capabilities, applications, and utility of space, coupled with a dramatic increase in the number of NRO customers and stakeholders.

The technology underpinning earth sensing was rapidly expanding, and the policy function was a critical focal point to define boundaries between the NRO, its customers, and its mission partners. This involved the policy team in negotiation of MOAs with other intelligence agencies about their relative roles and missions in the operation of near real-time systems. It also involved development of agreements delineating the boundary between NRO's intelligence missions and the roles and activities of organizations such as DARPA and the new Strategic Defense Initiative Organization. The policy staff also represented and protected NRO interests in supporting continuity of government initiatives.

Some of the key policy issues during this period involved pricing for shuttle launches and later the cost of the Space Station Freedom initiative. Those are good examples of how the NRO policy staff worked with NRO Staff alumni, now in key positions in other organizations, to help set national

---

[*]   A representative list of key events and policy documents is illustrated in the Timeline chart (inside back cover).

44

policies. Issues relative to pricing and cost for these NASA programs were worked through the National Security Council. Lt Cols Jim Morrell on the NRO Staff, Tom Maultsby in OSD Policy, and Dick McCormick, who was then on the IC Staff, worked as a team to get policies favorable to the NRP, while also protecting NRO equities, drafted and approved.

Many of the issues involving the NRO Staff policy team related to the boundary between the intelligence missions associated with reconnaissance and the military missions of surveillance and tactical operations. The CIA and Program B were highly focused on support to the President and Cabinet-level policy makers. Program C was highly focused on support to the operational Navy, and Program A was increasingly focused on support to military operations. The policy team was a critical element in managing the increasing importance and value of space capabilities to support military operations. This included support to TENCAP demonstrations and creation of the policy underpinnings for creation of the Defense Reconnaissance Support Program. Importantly, the policy team was the NRO lead organization in the planning for and the stand-up and development of new working relationships associated with the formation of Air Force Space Command and, subsequently, a Unified Command for space.

Launch

Unlike the acquisition, development, and funding of covert satellites, the launch of a satellite is a visible event that cannot be hidden. In the very early years after the NRO was established, a key issue was maintaining appropriate security, while living with the propensity of launches to fail. The Staff had an individual assigned to support the DNRO on launch issues– he tracked failures and recovery plans and interfaced with the NRO security team to deal with the security and cover stories for launches of NRO reconnaissance satellites.

In the late 1950s, all three services conducted space launches. However, by the early 1960s the Army's center of expertise, the Redstone Arsenal, was aligned with NASA as part of the Apollo mission to land men on the moon. The Navy focused on developing submarine-launched ICBMs, and satellite systems launched within DoD had become primarily the responsibility of the Air Force. Thus, the Air Force became the Department of Defense launch agent for essentially all NRO space launches.

In the early years, Program A, the Air Force component of the NRO, became the interface to the Air Force launch provider for launch of NRO satellites. Launch systems were tailored to the needs of the NRO satellites, and each booster was tagged to a specific satellite. The satellite developer, Program A's System Program Office (SPO), worked NRO launch interfaces and participated in the launch operation.

The advent of the Space Transportation System (STS), or Space Shuttle, during the mid-years of the NRO Staff, brought big changes to the launch process. The DoD agreed to launch all national security satellites on the Space Shuttle rather than on expendable launch vehicles. The NRO Staff Program Monitor's role was expanded to include a technical interface function to work with NASA and the Air Force on fielding the Space Shuttle, developing the infrastructure to support it, and redesigning the NRO satellites to optimize use of the Space Shuttle's larger cargo bay. Redesigning every satellite drove a very large increase in the NRP budget and increased competition for both missions and funding among the program offices.

By the time of the Reagan Administration, there was a National Policy decision to mandate use of the Space Shuttle for all US government satellites. Pete Aldridge (at the time both the DNRO and the Under Secretary of the Air Force) argued that total dependence on the shuttle before it had been proven was high risk and that the Air Force should invest in 10 additional Commercial (later

Complementary) Expendable Launch Vehicles* as an insurance policy in case of a shuttle accident. In this, the NRO Staff served as a personal staff to the Secretary/DNRO and interfaced with all organizations and agencies participating in launch policy and funding decisions.

The *Challenger* launch failure proved the wisdom of the back-up approach. The now-Secretary of the Air Force/DNRO Aldridge was the DoD leader in driving development of a new fleet of expendable launch vehicles to replace the shuttle, and the redesign of satellite missions from shuttle-only configurations to ELV-compatible designs. In this process, he worked with many elements of the Air Force and the DoD but relied heavily on the NRO Staff to provide personal staff support for development of decision papers and briefings, production of talking papers and guidance memos, and for fact finding and providing concise summaries of activities across the DoD.

The Early Years (1962–74). The NRO typically funded all NRO launches as a separate budget item from the satellite that was to be launched. In the early years, the Staff involvement included both a program monitoring role and a security protection role. The NRO/Air Force partnership for launch support was very strong from the beginning of the Thor/ launches of the Discoverer/Corona vehicles, and continuing through later Atlas/Agena (Gambit), Titan (Hexagon), and Sigint launches. By the time Brockway McMillan ended his tenure as DNRO, these launches had become fairly routine, notwithstanding the occasional failure, and thus required little NRO Staff engagement other than budget/funding issues.

At this time, launch failures were not uncommon, but since the satellites were planned for short operational lifetimes, and therefore essentially had production lines, a failure did not entail a substantial gap in mission coverage.

The NRO launch Program Element Monitor function existed from the very beginning of the NRO and was initially charged to provide security for movement of equipment to the launch ranges and for cover stories for NRO launches. Once the launches became "routine," and rather open secrets, the PEM function narrowed. During this period, the launch PEM's primary responsibilities were to provide staff support to the DNRO and represent the NRO in interactions with USAF, OSD, IC, Office of Management and Budget (OMB), and Congressional staff elements in areas including requirements and justification, budgeting, and launch schedule coordination.

Corona Launch - 25 May 1972

---

*   Initially CELV was the Commercial Launch Vehicle program but was later changed to the Complementary Launch Vehicle program due to political sensitivities.

46

During the latter part of this period, the scope of launch system-related activity on the Staff declined, and the launch PEM assumed additional responsibilities for representing and defending the NRO R&D investment program.

However, during this period DoD and the Air Force, as DoD Executive Agent for Manned Spaceflight, worked with NASA on the early stages of Space Shuttle planning and development. An MOA between NASA and the Air Force was signed in 1970 as NRO requirements were driving considerations on decisions about the size and capabilities of the shuttle. Preliminary commitments were made for DoD use of the shuttle, and DoD committed to reconfigure Space Launch Complex 6 (SLC-6, the former Dyna-Soar launch pad) at Vandenberg AFB, CA to serve as the west coast shuttle launch facility.

The Middle Years (1974–80). By the Carter Administration, the Space Shuttle development had reached a point where the DoD and NRO had to begin to take actions to transition from expendable launch vehicles to the shuttle. Dr. Hans Mark, as DNRO, reversed earlier guidance that NRO satellites had to be designed to be dual compatible with both shuttle* and expendable launch vehicles. His direction that all future NRO satellites would be optimized for the shuttle meant that they would no longer be compatible for launch on expendables.

To support the planning for transition to the Space Shuttle, a new position was created on the NRO Staff — the Deputy for shuttle planning — within the Policy and Security staff. This function had the responsibility to support the DNRO on needed decisions regarding shuttle transition, as well as to track progress and evolution of capabilities and procedures for the shuttle. Dr. Mark relied on this NRO Staff focal point, not only to advise him on NRO transition to the shuttle, but also broader Air Force activities related to launch transition. At this point, the NRO budget experienced a large increase because essentially all NRO programs had to be redesigned for the shuttle, and the non-recurring costs were large.

Within the redesign, the payloads were "shuttle optimized" – i.e. made wide and short, as the costs to the payload program office were based on the length of the shuttle bay. The Air Force also took on substantial investments to develop the Inertial Upper Stage (IUS) designed primarily for shuttle use, and to convert SLC-6 for shuttle launches. In both developments, the NRO had the driving requirements. The NRO also had requirements for security accommodations at NASA's Manned Spaceflight Center at Houston. The NRO Staff played a key role in negotiating these requirements with the Air Force and NASA.

During this time, Dr. Mark assigned Air Force Brig Gen Ralph Jacobson as a liaison officer at NASA Headquarters to coordinate shuttle issues. Brig Gen Jacobson, a former NRO officer, worked closely with the NRO Staff launch point of contact, as well as directly with Dr. Mark.

---

*   Interestingly, the sizing of the shuttle cargo bay was based on the NRO's Hexagon imaging satellite dimensions. The Hexagon, however, never flew on the Space Shuttle.

47

The Later Years (1980–90). The Reagan Administration's first National Space Policy (NSPD 8, 4 July 1982) endorsed the Carter Administration's decision that all military satellites would be optimized for launch on the shuttle.

By May 1983, National Security Decision Directive (NSDD) 94 encouraged development of a commercial expendable launch vehicle capability as a complement to the shuttle. This had the effect of providing a path to preserve the small and medium US expendable launch vehicle industry for commercial launch services. The subsequent policy in May 1984, which was promulgated as NSDD 144, required full cost recovery pricing for the shuttle, which showed the high cost of using the shuttle was non-competitive with commercial expendable launch. The Commercial Space Launch Act of October 1984 further encouraged the industry.

Then Air Force Secretary/DNRO Aldridge, and many senior Air Force officers, were concerned with the risks of becoming solely reliant on the Space Shuttle for access to space. They were also very concerned about the ballooning cost of shuttle launches, and the dim expectations that the shuttle would even be able to meet required NRO launch rates, much less reaching its advertised launch rate. DNRO Aldridge became a strong proponent for a change in policy that supported development of a commercial expendable capability, at least for long enough to gain experience and confidence in the shuttle launch program. It is important to recognize that because of the intense political interest and emotion regarding this debate, it required a significant amount of personal and political fortitude for the DNRO to take on this complex issue.

In making his argument, Mr. Aldridge relied heavily on the NRO Staff to gather information, draft briefings, assess options and costs, and perform analysis supporting his personal advocacy with the SECDEF, senior Administration policy makers, and the Congress. The Staff POC worked with NRO, NASA, and Air Force elements and, taking advantage of the streamlined staff structure, frequently worked directly with the DNRO. Brig Gen Tom Moorman, then the NRO Staff Director, would later comment, "During this period, no issue or subject had greater impact on the NRO Staff from a policy, budget, or technology perspective – one cannot over-emphasize the unique role the Staff played in the Shuttle transition."[44]

The *Challenger* failure in 1986 and subsequent shuttle stand-down of 32 months proved the need for a complementary launch capability. Coupled with two Titan 34D failures, as well as an Atlas and a Delta failure that occurred at about the same time, DoD had a serious space launch crisis.

NASA Space Shuttle *Discovery* Launch.

Secretary/DNRO Aldridge had taken the lead for DoD in shuttle transition issues and was a very hands-on leader driving decisions and funding for redesigning satellites for ELV compatibility. After *Challenger*, he also drove funding completion of the 10 CELVs that had been authorized but not yet assembled, monitoring the Titan 34D accident investigations, and starting up production on new medium and heavy-lift boosters.

In this work, DNRO Aldridge relied on the NRO Staff, working along with the Air Force Program Office, to support him as his personal staff to work on the range of launch issues that extended far beyond the NRO's normal equities. This approach provided him with information and assessments on activities throughout both DoD and the contractor community. It quickly provided him with cost estimates and risk assessments, bypassing intermediate Air Force staffs. The NRO Staff developed briefings and coordinated extensively with the launch SPO, the Space and Missile Systems commander, and other senior launch decision makers. The NRO Staff Director, Brig Gen Moorman, facilitated and directed many of these senior-level deliberations.

Mr. Edward C. Aldridge, Jr.
DNRO: 3 Aug 1981 - 16 Dec 1988

The NRO Staff also worked with other elements of the Air Force who themselves reported to Secretary/DNRO Aldridge on space launch recovery issues. Included among these was Major General Don Kutyna, Air Force Space and Missile Center (SMC) Deputy Commander for Launch Systems and the senior Air Force representative on the Rogers (*Challenger*) Commission. The Air Force Mission Area Director for Space and Air Force legal staffs, who were implementing the Commercial Space Launch Act, also participated in discussions. Finally, the SAF/Space Policy Office, representing DoD in NSC Space Policy, was also involved.

> "I came in as Under Secretary and DNRO in August 1981 and stayed there until December 1988. The NRO Staff played a unique role during this period, performing a much more expansive role for the combined activities of the Under Secretary, Secretary, and DNRO.
>
> Why did the NRO Staff take on this expanded role in 1981? Except for the launch crews and the acquisition expertise in El Segundo… the depth of space expertise in the Air Force was "shallow." Therefore, the NRO Staff filled this void."[45]
>
> — DNRO Pete Aldridge

Within the larger context of this history, there is no better example of the benefits of the streamlined management and selective staffing that characterized the NRO Staff than the advisory role that it played to the DNRO on the most important issue in his time in the position.

49

Budget and Legislative Liaison

The DNRO managed and administrated a single consolidated National Reconnaissance Program that funded all NRO activities including studies, development, launch, and operations. The financial management function included whatever coordination and justification that was required with the Executive and Congressional budget processes. The process established was highly streamlined, with waivers granted to many standard oversight and regulatory processes. The NRP was reviewed by a small group of cleared personnel and then was incorporated and "fenced" within the Air Force budget to protect knowledge of both its size and existence.

The criticality and sensitivity of the NRP-funded programs led to the decisions to incrementally fund activities. Thus, rather than having to precisely define and fully fund a new program before it started, the NRP provided only the funds required for that budget year. This provided the flexibility to incorporate evolving technology to improve a satellite's performance and lifetime. This also smoothed the NRP budget and avoided the need for peaks and valleys associated with including all the funds that would be expended over several years in just one year. They maintained a termination reserve that protected against the decision to terminate a program once it was underway. Another feature was the use on "no year" money. In most DoD programs, different types of expenditures, once appropriated, must either be expended or they expire within a specified period of years and are turned back to the Treasurer. The ability to carry forward funds from year-to-year was critical in the early years when many satellites/boosters failed. The flexibility provided by funds carried forward from prior years allowed quick response without suffering the delays and complexity of getting supplemental funds through Congress.

In later years, several other budget programs, designed to provide supplemental funds from DoD to fund studies, experiments, and new capabilities, specifically focused on support to military operations. These programs (e.g. TENCAP, DRSP) were managed in coordination, but separately from the NRP and the NRO Staff.[46]

> "I remember the "rack and stack" budget drill that we did every year in the 4C-1000 conference room with Jimmie Hill. When we were done, we would call in Pete Aldridge and Jimmie would summarize the results for his approval. After that we would produce the Congressional Budget Justification Book and send it to the CIA printing office for publication and delivery to the Congress. We would "practice" with the DNRO to prepare him for his congressional testimony. We would offer example questions that the DNRO might get in the hearings and critique the DNRO response in real-time. We were diplomatic in our constructive criticism. I always enjoyed that part of the staff's function. The bottom line for the staff was to "get the money" for the programs."[47]
>
> — Brig Gen Donald Walker,
> NRO Staff Director, 1989-92

The Early Years (1962–74). When the NRO was established, financial management was one of the major points of controversy between the CIA and the NRO. DCI John McCone, for example, recommended that all funds necessary for the CIA to execute covert satellite projects be released directly to the CIA. Dr. Joseph Charyk countered in a memo to Roswell Gilpatric, Robert McNamara's deputy, that "if the NRO is to function it must be responsible for continuous monitoring of financial and technical program status, must control the release of funds to programs, and must be able to reallocate [funds] between NRP programs."[48] In an interview with Dr. Charyk in September 2014, he recalled insisting that the NRO had to review and control program budgets and key technical decisions for a *national* covert space program to be successful.[49]

The final result was that the funding to support all NRO programs was consolidated into a single budget known as the National Reconnaissance Program which was administrated by the DNRO.

For the first 14 years after formation of the NRO, budget formulation and monitoring was executed by the NRO's chief financial officer. This was a GS-17 position detailed from the CIA that reported directly to the Director of the NRO. He was supported by a staff of two Air Force officers plus a secretary <u>and</u> worked in parallel and close coordination with the NRO Staff. He attended EXCOM meetings and would often represent the DNRO on budget matters which were annually approved in December and reviewed quarterly.*

The NRO had only two chief financial officers. John Holleran who served from 1961 until his retirement in 1974 was often characterized as carrying everything you would want to know about the NRO in his pocket. Jimmie Hill, who replaced him, had an incredible memory and carried it all in his head. Hill served as chief financial officer from 1974–1978 and went on to be Staff Director and Deputy Director of the NRO. In coordination with the Program Directors and their Service/Agency financial elements, the chief financial officer and his small staff integrated the annual budget. They coordinated with the few cleared financial management interfaces in OSD and OMB and presented the budget to the few cleared members of Congress. They subsequently managed distribution of appropriations to the programs. By the late 1970s, the financial staff functions were divided between Lt Col Dave Doyle who worked the annual budget allocation and Lt Col Chuck Gyauch who was responsible for the five-year projections and TENCAP interfaces, as well as the Congressional and OMB interfaces.[50]

The Middle Years (1974–80). DNRO Hans Mark reorganized the budget process in 1978. By that time the budget oversight processes had changed. The EXCOM had been disestablished, and the Intelligence Oversight Committees were formed in Congress. The Director of CIA had been given the additional duty of Director of Central Intelligence and responsibility for management of the National Foreign Intelligence Program (NFIP), including the NRP. The IC Staff was established, separate and apart from the CIA, to support him in exercising his community duties.

Dr. Mark abolished the position of chief financial officer. In its place he established an Office of Programs and Budget within the NRO Staff. This office consisted of eight Air Force officers, one CIA officer, and three secretaries, a substantial increase from its earlier staffing.

A major function of this new Staff element was the preparation and justification of the NRP to the larger oversight process including the IC Staff and Congress. The IC Staff and both Congressional Committees established new oversight processes with program/budget monitors dedicated to oversight of the NRP.

---

* The chief financial officer (John Holleran) is remembered for his white socks and the notebook that he carried in his back pocket. The notebook contained all the details of the NRP budget.

51

The Programs and Budget Office provided the primary liaison between the NRO and the new budget oversight functions of the IC Staff and the Congressional Committees. It was the Staff POC for developing, coordinating, and publishing an annual Congressional Budget Justification Book. It built and monitored the budget for the NRP and later, the DRSP. Within the budget office, individuals were assigned from Programs A, B, and C. Each program had a single person responsible for tracking the program dollars, overseeing that the technical staff fully justified the funds required for their activities, and ensuring that budget requests were accurate, budgets were dispersed to the programs accurately, and expenditure schedules stayed on track. There was close coordination and work allocation within the NRO Staff, especially among Budget staff and the Program Element Monitors.

With Congress assuming a much larger and more detailed role in overseeing the NRP, a full-time position for Legislative Affairs was established within the existing NRO Budget Office in 1978, reporting to the Director for Programs and Budget. This legislative liaison function increased in scope and importance throughout the remainder of the time the NRO Staff existed. This individual maintained a close working relationship with the technical staff, as well as the Staff Director and the DDNRO, and oversaw the CBJB process. A tremendous *esprit de corps* existed among the Staff. While everyone advocated for their own program office, a deep respect for other Staff members and their programs existed. The NRO Legislative Affairs officer also had close relationships with the directors of Programs A, B, and C, as well as the directors of the individual system program offices. In many ways, the Legislative Affairs function provided the glue between the programs and Capitol Hill.

The Later Years (1980-90). External oversight continued to expand, but the NRO's financial flexibility with incremental funding and the ability to carry forward unspent funds was preserved. This flexibility proved crucial in 1986, for example, after an NRO payload exploded at Vandenberg (80 days after *Challenger*) and the debris not only damaged the SLC-4E launch platform, but it also damaged the -4W pad downrange. The accident left a gaping hole in West Coast launch capability, with the critical launch of an essential new satellite scheduled in six months. The NRO applied the Carry Forward funds to repair both launch pads, enabling the autumn launch to proceed on schedule. Without this flexibility, the timely launch would not have been possible.

The leadership of Mr. Jimmie Hill, as both Staff Director and later as DDNRO, was a critical factor in the NRO's success. His phenomenal memory, aptitude for resource management, demonstrated integrity, and sense of fairness earned him tremendous respect in the Community. With support from the NRO Staff, he was a force to be reckoned with and one from which to learn. He influenced all major decisions and Congressional actions related to the NRO.

The quality of the NRO budget process is reflected in quotes from key internal and external leaders of this era. Former SSCI Staff Budget Director, and later NRO Director, Keith Hall commented on his experiences on the Hill:

> The NRO Legislative Liaison staff was at the top of the pack. [They] never shaded the truth. Without a doubt some of the issues were concluded to the benefit of the NRO because of the direct involvement of the NRO Staff. The work in the trenches by the Staff, and with Jimmie Hill as the final arbiter, served the NRO well. There were always big issues with the NRO each year because that was where the money was. Other Intelligence Community elements never lacked ammunition against the NRO. They tried to find issues with the programs. Some were envious of the

Mr. Keith R. Hall
DNRO: 28 Mar 1997 - 13 Dec 2001

budget. The NSA Legislative Liaison team was more like cheerleaders than NRO. It is said that our government is based on a separation of powers. When there is an issue between the two, it is more like a collision of powers. A good legislative liaison shop helps "cushion the blow." In his early days on the Hill, the CIA Legislative Liaison often tried to accelerate the collision. NSA and CIA sometimes made issues personal. This was not the case with the NRO. Greg [Gilles] and Joanne [Isham] helped to explain where the Hill was coming from on an issue and why. Sometimes though, the program would burst into flames anyway. Nevertheless, they tried to explain the Hill's position and even if it was unreasonable, they tried to calm people down and reduce the friction. They were usually successful at that, no matter how hot the issue was.[51]

Communications

The NRO's highly covert mission required high performance, tailored communications for administrative, and in particular, operational mission support. The origins of the NRO communications functions can be traced back to a 1964 declassified memorandum signed by Brig Gen John L. Martin, Jr., the NRO Staff Director, in which he described the duties of the NRO Communications Officer to include advising the NRO Staff Director of:

> All matters having a significant impact on NRO communications, as well as providing staff action [for] all communications matters referred to the DNRO for consideration. By 1964 this role had expanded to include... [to] provide communications services for the NRO... arrange for: leasing or procurement of circuits and equipment; manpower authorizations and properly cleared/trained personnel to operate and maintain NRO communications facilities.... Supervise communications security for USAF-operated NRO communications facilities and develop a high level of security consciousness, knowledge, and discipline at each communications center.[52]

Initially, the NRO relied on messages sent by teletype from communications center to communications center. "Comm centers" were established at Byeman facilities, and a dedicated Special Operations Communications network or SOCOM was established. As requirements for connectivity expanded, the NRO communications support grew to include hundreds of dedicated communications personnel, specially managed through the Air Force to provide secure connectivity among government, contractor, and user organizations.

> DNRO Pete Aldridge invited Casper Weinberger, the Secretary of Defense, to come to his office for a demonstration. After making a call the SECDEF, noticeably irritated, asked the question "Why can't the regular DoD systems have a capability this easy to use and with voice recognition quality?" Shortly thereafter, the DoD initiated the RED Switch program that supported DoD-wide secure voice for the services and Unified and Specified Commands.
>
> — Maj Gen Phil Bracher, USAF (Ret.)

53

The staff communicator's role was to help define and to coordinate requirements and budget and to ensure communications operations supported the organization's needs. The staff POC also held a position on the Air Force staff, enabling him to coordinate communications and influence budget, development, and resource allocation decisions to support NRO needs. He also had a third job as commander of the line organization supporting NRO communications.

Consistent with the NRO approach, the line organization supporting the NRO was designed to manage systems from cradle-to-grave with selective manning similar to that enjoyed by the Air Force personnel assigned to the NRO. It drew on the Air Force for standard equipment but also developed, as well as operated, new advanced technology systems. The line organization began as a 12-person detachment commanded by an Air Force captain but evolved into Squadrons, Groups, and finally into a single Air Force Communications Wing of over one thousand military and contractor personnel, with an operating budget of nearly $500,000 and supporting assets of $5 Billion.[53] It developed and fielded leading edge advances in secure voice and message handling, facsimile capabilities, and secure tactical dissemination systems. It also enabled the NRO to be the earliest national security adopter of commercial long-line services and at the forefront in the secure application of new digital applications, internet services, and email. Many of these NRO-led capabilities were subsequently adopted by DoD and government agencies, such as the White House Communications Agency, the State Department, and other government agencies.

The Early Years (1962–74). The initial 4C-1000 communications team of twelve Air Force communicators operated a special communications center, providing classified and unclassified communications services. The senior communications officer, Captain Jones, was assigned overtly to DCS/Operations, Hq Air Force Communications Service, but covertly and functionally to the NRO Staff Executive Officer, Lt Col Van Mater. Day-to-day, the team was responsible for providing communications and data transmission services in support of all NRP satellite operations assigned to the Satellite Operations Center, as well as to the entire NRO Staff and DNRO.[54]

Two years later, Brig Gen Martin's replacement, Brig Gen David Bradburn, issued a similar memorandum with more emphasis and detail on the commander's supervisory line responsibilities within the communications center, but at the same time, changing his NRO Staff point of contact to that of the Deputy Director for Plans and Policy, continuing to emphasize his staff role, but also adding emphasis to his supervisory role in operating the communications center:

> In addition to the NRO Staff functional responsibilities provided to [the DNRO], I recognize that the NRO Communications Officer fills a unique role in support of the NRO. As in the past, I desire that the NRO Staff point of contact for the NRO Communications Officer be the Deputy Director for Plans and Policy….[to] provide communications services for the NRO.….arrange for: leasing or procurement of circuits and equipment; manpower authorizations; and properly cleared/trained personnel to operate and maintain NRO communications facilities….Supervise communications security for USAF-operated NRO communications facilities and develop a high level of security consciousness, knowledge, and discipline at each communications center….Provide frequent briefings to the Deputy Director for Plans and Policy, NRO staff, on the overall status, and plans for, the NRO Communications network.[55]

The key component of the NRO Communications infrastructure during this period was the Special Operations Communications network or SOCOM. It was based on the standard Air Force hard-copy messaging system but with unique security keying for the NRO. In its early years, the network was comprised of a torn-tape relay hub centered in the Pentagon basement, connected

54

via communications lines to key NRO facilities. During this period, the SOCOM system expanded to support all elements of the NRO, its ground stations, and contractor base. It was also used to support product information flow to some high priority users. SOCOM was not the only communications capability of NRO communications. From the outset, NRO provided secure voice communications and facsimile transmission capabilities in support of both operational and administrative traffic. In the earliest days, secure voice communications were serviced by the DoD's Automatic Secure Voice Communications network (AUTOSEVOCOM). Facsimile was connected through the secure voice line to provide very low-rate but secure support, particularly for small facilities not serviced by SOCOM.

The Middle Years (1974–80). This period saw the continued growth in communications support for the NRO with new detachments supporting the growing NRO infrastructure. Close coordination between NRO program planning and communications planning were essential.

There was a strong desire for improved secure voice and facsimile capabilities. The NRO communicators worked closely with NSA to help fund and expedite the development of advanced technology devices such as the Secure Telephone Unit (STU)-I and STU-II. They also contracted for development of new light-weight fax machines to operate with the STU devices to provide improved capability. The combination of secure voice and secure facsimile provided essential communications capability to smaller contractors and NRO outposts, as well as the ability to establish temporary operating sites.

COMMANDER'S CONFERENCE 13 SEPTEMBER 1977
FRONT ROW: TSgt Stults, Capt Tempel, Maj Bracher, CMSgt Cyprych, Don Jewell. SECOND ROW: Jean Abney, CMSgt Spaar, SMSgt Curtis, MSgt Young. THIRD ROW: MSgt Snow, TSgt Ratliff, SMSgt Pannell, MSgt Aguilar. FOURTH ROW: TSgt Tarpening, CMSgt Cowart, MSgt Garland. FIFTH ROW: TSgt Paulk, MSgt Shultz, MSgt Vick, MSgt Funk. SIXTH ROW: SMSgt McCoy, CMSgt Williams, TSgt Quinn, MSgt Jilg. SEVENTH ROW: Capt Kraus, TSgt Shelton, TSgt Stewart, MSgt Leighow, MSgt Book, SSgt Landry.

55

One of the major accomplishments was the development and stand-up of the Defense Dissemination System (DDS), which enabled near real-time imagery to flow to operational users worldwide. A new dedicated squadron that was established to support this effort included operational testing, as well as 24-hour-a-day operations.

During this period, the NRO's communications support elements began to also support a few other very high priority compartmented programs. The NRO staff POC coordinated these efforts with support to the NRO to ensure there was no degradation in service to the NRO.

As an example of not only the quality of the people assigned to the NRO, but also the staffing priority given to NRO Communications, Major Phil Bracher was assigned as the multi-hatted NRO Staff senior communicator in 1977 as a major. He left the Staff in 1985 as a colonel after coordinating a major expansion and modernization of communications capabilities. He led the line organization through a Squadron to Group level expansion and led planning for what eventually evolved into an Air Force Communications Wing, which all grew from a modest twelve-person NRO communications unit in the basement of the Pentagon.[*]

The Later Years (1980–90). The 1980s was the beginning of a revolution in communications, and the NRO was at the forefront in adopting new technologies. NRO communications were early adopters of new high-speed long lines and satellite links that were becoming commercially available. They pioneered the development and installation of a high speed, totally integrated digital switch. This was the first operational CONUS-wide digital switch within the government that integrated both secure voice and computer data traffic and served thousands of subscribers.

They adapted the secure red phone system, then in use by the NRO and based initially on STU-II and then STU-III technology, to the much higher bandwidths enabled by the broadband lines and digital switches to provide a greatly improved secure voice and facsimile capability for the NRO.

By the mid-1980s the requirement for NRO secure tactical communications had grown to the point that field users wanted more and quicker data services. The NRO communications team developed and fielded a highly portable, light-weight satellite terminal that would operate on the Defense Satellite Communications System (DSCS). This was a huge success and was adopted for use by the White House Communications Agency and also, in different variants, by the services, the Unified and Specified commands, and the commercial communication satellites used by news organizations.

The NRO started beta testing secure email in the mid-1980s. At first it was hosted as an application on the SOCOM computers, so it was limited to sites that hosted a SOCOM relay. Users accessed their email account via remote computer terminals hard-wired to SOCOM computers. As the commercial markets grew, the email applications were ported to desktop computers by 1990.

While secure and responsive communications continued to be a significant feature of NRO infrastructure, with the consolidation of NRO program offices in January 1993, the NRO communications office became fully integrated into the NRO organizational structure as the Communications Systems Directorate (COMM - one of the three original NRO Directorates), created to direct policy and to oversee the security and control of all NRO space and ground-based communications systems.

---

[*] Maj Gen Bracher retired from the Air Force in 1995.

Technology

In the aggregate, technology development in the NRO was the product of teamwork between the NRO technology offices, program office SPOs, NRO contractors, government laboratories, and the NRO Staff technology group. However, during the early days of the NRO, technology development was often accomplished with little technology management structure. The Quill satellite program, for example, fielded a spaceborne platform from a collection of basic technologies that had essentially been developed for airborne systems and adapted to the space environment. The basic Quill technologies were developed by a consortium of NRO program offices.

According to Donald Regenhardt, assigned to the Staff in the late 1960s as, at the time, the lone technology staff officer who managed what was then referred to as the Applied Research (AR) and Advanced Technology (AT) budget lines, there was a minimum of process in centrally managing the NRO technologies. He managed the technology lines for the DNRO, working directly with Col Lew Allen in Program A and Mr. Les Dirks in Program B, both later to become senior NRO leaders.*This was during the period of intense competition between the two program offices for the next generation imaging system, the Program A FROG system or the Program B electro-optical imagery system. The allocation of AR/AT funds was generally made on a case-by-case basis, the NRO chief financial officer managed the financial process with line-in/line-out entries in his pocket notebook. Regenhardt recalled the preponderance of Program A funding requests being approved (including at least one individual FROG related request). Program B generally self-funded their technology, although openly sharing the technology program details with Regenhardt. That changed when Brig Gen Allen came to the Staff as Director, encouraging a more equitable distribution of NRO technology funds amongst the program offices. The early years in particular, despite program office rivalries, were characterized by exceptional cross-program technology sharing.[56]

The NRO Staff technology group represented the program offices in prioritizing NRO technology initiatives across the NRO, eliminating duplication of effort, coordinating cross-program technology use, developing the Congressional Budget Justification Book submittal for technology, and as appropriate, managing technology transfer functions to external organizations.

The NRO Staff designed a much more *structured* R&D process in the early 1980s to encourage contractors, government laboratories, and NRO program offices to efficiently develop and mature technologies with applications unique to spaceborne NRO reconnaissance systems.

This new process recognized technology development within the individual program offices and external technology centers, distinguishing between more basic and applied technology research, as well as advanced system development. This structured process removed much of the personality-driven aspects of identifying key technologies to more of an NRO-wide, requirements-driven process. This structured process began to focus more on the NRO operational requirements than just a technology driven set of R&D projects. This new process also helped win Congressional approval of a more "requirements driven" process which they preferred.[57]

At the heart of this NRO Staff-managed technology program were the Reconnaissance Technology (RT) program (basic and applied research) and the Advanced Development (AD) program (advanced technical development). Both programs resulted from a recognized need for a formal and sustained R&D program with a means to flow down technology priorities for development. These two programs were administered by the NRO Staff and executed through the technology offices in the three NRO program offices. Historically, roughly 80% of the funds were allocated directly to the program offices

---

   *   Mr. Les Dirks became the Director of the Office of Development & Engineering (Program B), and General Lew Allen became the Director of the NRO Staff, and later the Air Force Chief of Staff.

57

for the approved projects, and the remainder was held back by the NRO Staff to be competed for best-of-breed program submissions. Although the history of how the percentage of RT/AD funding was established and allocated has been remembered differently by various NRO technology chiefs, generally Program A received about 40-50%, Program B received 35%, and Program C was allocated the remainder.[58] It should be noted that this Staff-administered process was one of the few in which the NRO Staff had a direct and defined resource management role, adjudicating in this case between program office technology solutions. It should be noted that while the Staff had responsibility for allocating funds between the Reconnaissance Technology lines, in the later years the DDNRO traditionally provided ultimate approval of the annual NRO technology program.

Generally, the Staff promoted effective coordination between program offices on RT—formally at the RT/AD reviews and informally at the R&D off-sites hosted by the NRO technology staff. In the early years, the program offices were very open, and their technology development efforts were freely shared. The Staff Technologists provided guidance and adjudicated any duplication of effort. In later years, however, the cross-program reviews became much more adversarial and politically charged, just as program offices battled for a greater share of resources.

In spite of the competitive efforts between the technology groups, there were many positive examples of Staff coordination and brokering between program offices to minimize unnecessary duplication of effort. Random examples included the Common Data Transmission Study and implementation, control moment gyro (CMG) development, image processing and advanced media development, advances in laser diodes, focal plane array optimization, solar cell efficiency advancements, on-board recorder upgrades, and low noise amplifier upgrades, just to name a few.

Not all NRO R&D was performed under the RT/AD rubric. The Photo Configuration Control Board (PCCB), for example, addressed the unique technology requirements of the imagery community. The board and budget were managed by the NRO Staff. The board chairman was rotated between Programs A and B, and Program A handled the contractual actions. The PCCB became a model for cross-program managed projects in the imagery film and digital processing domains. Major successes spawned from the PCCB included advanced microdensitometer and Visual Edge Matching machines for measuring image quality, as well as development of ultra-ultra-thin-base films and chemistry. Probably the most significant attribute of the PCCB was that highly competitive NRO representatives supported the board-managed programs; consensus was reached on virtually all technology projects. Separate but related to the PCCB, the NRO film and chemistry contract covered the operation and maintenance of the Eastman Kodak production of NRO film and processing chemistry. Management of the contract, a line rather than a traditional staff function, nevertheless was administered by the NRO Staff, a perceived neutral entity within the broader NRO organization.[59]

The Staff technology office, like many other Staff elements, was also a responsive resource for the DNRO in directly supporting the Director in his DNRO hat, while at other times supporting him in his SECAF hat, which often enabled him to deal with complex national security issues without the burdensome bureaucratic coordination requirements inherent in traditional government staffs. For example, in the mid-1980s the SECDEF requested DNRO Pete Aldridge to evaluate whether adding significant funding could significantly accelerate the Ballistic Missile Defense (BMD) program. After reviewing operational NRO programs, major block changes, and the technology development profiles from the NRO's robust technology driven program, the Staff quickly produced five slides the SECDEF was able to use with the BMD program office (BMDO) and the President to demonstrate that large increases in the BMDO budget would do little to accelerate the program because of the technology development timelines required. The DNRO input, supported largely by the NRO Staff's assessment, ultimately drove the national security decision.

58

Program Formulation and Monitoring

Traditionally, the functions of Program Element Monitors are performed by all the military departments. These PEMs, assigned to headquarters staffs are responsible for representing the acquisition or operational element within the headquarters, while at the same time, representing the System Program Office in the field.

The NRO PEM function was a core element of the NRO Staff. The key differential between NRO PEMs and those in the Military Departments, however, was the NRO streamlined management environment in which the NRO PEM operated. While a Service PEM had multiple levels of supervision, the NRO PEMs were much more empowered to interact directly with senior decision makers, including the DNRO, national intelligence agency leaders, and Congress. They were also responsible for keeping their program office informed about the Washington community. Each NRO PEM was expected to provide a depth of knowledge about "their satellite's" funding, design, schedule, capability, mission objectives, and other programmatic factors. They were also required to exercise judgment in balancing the role of program advocate and the role of providing impartial Staff advice to the DNRO.

PEMs were selected based on an agreement between the Staff Director and the particular Program Director, and they derived authority and empowerment from each. From the beginning, Program A, which was located 2,500 miles and three time zones from Washington, chose and empowered very qualified PEMs who were often officers earmarked for jobs of increased responsibility in the future. However, in the early years the CIA and Navy programs, which were both located in the Washington area, did not provide the NRO Staff with similarly qualified PEMs. Instead they sought to represent programs from their headquarters. Program C filled the PEM role with operations officers, while the CIA often assigned officers who had limited specific knowledge of the satellite programs they represented. For periods of time, their PEM positions were not filled, and Air Force officers were assigned to cover the function. Initially both the Navy and CIA viewed the NRO Staff PEM as nothing more than a communications path between the program office and Staff. The CIA perception changed in the mid-1980s, and from that time forward they also selected and empowered highly qualified and upwardly mobile PEMs.[60] In the early years, the airborne reconnaissance programs managed by Program D were represented on the Staff as a parallel office, equivalent to but separate from the NRO Staff's space-related activities.

Once assigned, the PEMs generally had little supervision and were expected to develop the appropriate relationships, maintain their system knowledge, and to be prepared to address whatever program issues that might arise. Characteristic of most other NRO Staff officers, program element monitors operated with an extreme level of empowerment, uncharacteristic of individuals in other government staffs.

59

USAF Captain Jim Hoskins, a SIGINT Program Element Monitor in the late 1980s, recalled an incident on a late Friday afternoon while visiting an office in the basement of the Pentagon. Mr. Hill's exec called down and told him that "Jimmie" wanted to see him ASAP to discuss his program's architecture. Jim returned to his office and pulled out three vu-graphs from his safe. When he opened the door to Mr. Hill's office it was pitch dark. Around the table was the head of Space Command, a four-star general, accompanied by a three-star. There was a vu-graph machine on the table. Mr. Hill introduced Jim, who was customarily dressed in civilian clothes, as his expert on the program being discussed. He explained they were discussing whether one program with slight modification could satisfy an urgent Air Force need. Jim convincingly argued that it could. Mr. Hill then said "Gentlemen, the meeting is over" and told the Air Force they had gotten the answer. Jim later learned that the four-star wanted an immediate decision to de-stack one NRO satellite on the launch pad to accelerate the launch of the Air Force system. Obviously, de-stacking would have caused a nine-month delay and major expense.[61]

The Early Years (1962–74). The issues in the early years were primarily technical. Technology, rather than budget, was the primary constraint. When several system design options were identified, they were often treated as risk mitigation and funded. As previously noted, the stakeholder community in the early years was small and limited to only a few advisors to the President and very senior members of the OSD and Intelligence Community — virtually no oversight staff was cleared. Interactions with the Congress were limited to a few Committee Chairmen, and interactions were largely limited to NRO leadership. PEMs typically provided deep technical knowledge and supported the DNRO in his interactions with his peers and seniors. When the EXCOM was formed, the PEMs drafted status reports and information briefings to the Committee. The PEM function was to support the DNRO in his management of the technical aspects of the programs and to prepare him for his interactions with those other players. As the number of programs was small and the number of players was small, the PEM staff was very small. In some instances, where the technology and missions were comparable, one person covered two or more programs.

Space technology advanced rapidly in the 1960s and early 70s, and it became feasible for NRO systems to address a broader array of intelligence needs and users. When the EXCOM established sub-committees to assess program options, the PEM role expanded to include participation in EXCOM committee deliberations and support to EXCOM-directed studies.

In addition to normal staffing functions, two key programmatic issues occupied selected PEMs during the early years. One particular issue involved assessing and selecting between two competing technical solutions for providing time-sensitive imagery. The challenge was to avoid future operational surprises, such as the Soviet Union's invasion of Czechoslovakia. A second issue related to the new and critical national security intelligence gap concerning the Soviet anti-ballistic missile threat. Three technical solutions were offered, each addressing a different aspect of the problem. Following internal and community studies, the decision was made to acquire all three systems. These studies led to an increase in the number of stakeholders and the expansion of the PEM role from predominantly internal to a larger stakeholder support role. This was the last time that technical feasibility alone was the key issue. Future system trade studies focused more on cost effectiveness, the High-Altitude Sigint study being a case in point.

60

The Middle Years (1974–80). As noted earlier, the intelligence reorganizations and fallout from the Church and Pike Commissions resulted in termination of the EXCOM and creation of congressional Select Committees to oversee the Intelligence Community. Coupled with the Carter Administration's establishment of a DCI-led Intelligence Community Staff, this new oversight led to an expanded set of NRO PEM responsibilities. The number of individuals performing the PEM role continued to be nominally one person for each major program. However, while PEMs were still required to have a solid understanding of their program, the selection focus became less on deep technical knowledge and more on interpersonal skills and an understanding of the mission requirements, capabilities, and the intelligence user community.

The DNROs in this period, Dr. Hans Mark and his successor, Dr. Bob Hermann, were very hands-on managers. When they had questions, they would seek out the most knowledgeable person and would frequently walk into a PEM's office with a question or with guidance to be passed on to the program office.

The PEMs continued to be responsible for assisting the DNRO, DDNRO, and Staff Director with their decisions and their increasing interactions with the Congress, IC Staff, Intelligence Agency seniors, and OSD. PEMs also continued to work with NSA, DIA, DMA, and other agencies. TENCAP, the DRSP, and expanded NRO Staff elements dealing with policy, budget, and congressional relations all created the need for PEMs to coordinate their activities and their programs more broadly across the Staff. For example, during this time a PEM and an NRO Policy staff member jointly represented the DNRO in negotiating an MOA with NSA that resolved conflicts between agency charters and established lines of responsibility between the two agencies. It also consolidated the NRO and NSA operational tasking elements and established a position for an NSA representative detailed to serve on the NRO Staff.

The intelligence community reorganization during this time resulted in an increase in oversight by not only the Congress, but also the White House, the Intelligence Community, the Department of Defense, and other intelligence agency users. The PEMs interacted extensively with HPSCI and SSCI committee staffs to explain and justify programs and funding requirements. As Congressional requests expanded, the PEMs became responsible for drafting program sections of the annual Congressional Budget Justification Book. The IC Staff, established under the DCI, undertook to lead a number of system studies to assess options and costs for transition of NRO programs to the Space Shuttle. PEMs often served as the interface between the NRO, the program offices, and the IC study groups, providing analysis and developing options for assessment. The PEMs also worked with the OSD staff where participation had increased to include a policy team from USD (Policy) and a technical team (ASD/C3I). These organizations both participated in IC studies and performed independent analysis to counter the IC Staff positions. The people staffing these organizations, including the White House and Congressional staff, were often NRO alumni and asked very informed questions.

The introduction of zero-based budgeting and efforts to reduce defense and intelligence budgets led to a number of hard program choices that put pressure on the PEMs to defend programmatic elements and to be sufficiently knowledgeable of budget, expenditures, and IC needs to offer performance options when fallout funding did become available.

> USAF Capt. Jim Beale, a SIGINT Program Element Monitor in the late 1970s, recalled his role in the Elint mix decision, "Dr. Hermann tasked me to represent the NRO on the DCI's Sigint Mix study. Over several months, I worked with the IC Staff-led/ Community team and served as an interface with the two program offices. At the end of the study I briefed Dr. Hermann and NRO Senior Staff on the results which led to his decision to include the evolutionary approach in his proposed budget. When the decision was eventually passed to the President's Science Advisor, I was tasked to present the DNROs recommended program and rationale. Throughout the process, I was probably three ranks junior to the people I was working with."[62]

Another event that impacted the PEM function during this period was a DCI decision to cancel a Program B satellite program part way through development. The budget action came as a surprise to the Director of Program B and led to his decision to view the NRO Staff PEM position as a key job. From that time forward with few exceptions, the CIA assigned highly qualified program experts, instead of people with less specific program knowledge, to the PEM role.

Also, in 1978 the NRO Satellite Operations Center was disestablished, and from that time forward the PEMs assumed the additional responsibility to represent the NRO on COMIREX and the SIGINT Committee and to support the development of long-term guidance. They also became the most immediately available person to answer DNRO questions about the operational status of programs.

The Later Years (1980–90). The DNRO during the Reagan Administration, Pete Aldridge, was a very engaged leader. At that time, the number of PEMs was still typically one person for each major program/activity, but there were more activities and thus a few more PEMs. The NRO continued to be very streamlined with the DNRO and DDNRO working directly with junior Staff members.

By 1981, the community involved with NRO programs had expanded dramatically, and throughout this period the number of cleared and involved people continued to grow. The scope of PEM responsibilities grew with the number of issues, but as the issues increasingly involved more than one NRO activity, users would often find themselves working with several different NRO PEMs. Maintaining a common NRO voice became increasingly difficult.

In addition to providing staff support for the DNRO and interacting with the intelligence community, the PEMs were the focal point for programmatic details and program options to the expanding user community. This included programmatic support and impact analysis for those seeking to expand support to military operations, such as the staffs in TENCAP, DRSP, and service staffs. They also worked with OSD on elements of the Strategic Defense Initiative, including issues regarding potential NRO support and the potential for shared technology.

The PEMs also provided an interface between those working Continuity of Government initiatives and the NRO SPO's assessments of system options, both for supporting the initiative and for enhanced satellite system survivability. Often survivability came at a cost to performance, creating tough trades between advocates for better performance, or new requirements, and those concerned with the availability of systems from a continuity of operations perspective.

Internal competition between NRO Programs A, B, and C and their system program offices created serious challenges for PEMs in this era. The *Challenger* disaster, which is discussed elsewhere in this monograph, was a major driver in many ways influencing the PEMs' focus and workload. However, maintaining a single NRO voice became increasingly difficult as PEMs for different programs were pressured to advocate for their programs' proposed investment options.

These systemic NRO problems, which had been manageable in the early and mid-years of the NRO Staff became increasingly difficult to deal with in the later years when a much broader community of users, more capable and expensive systems, and more inclusive decision processes became the norm.

Studies, Plans, and Analysis

Looking across the history of the NRO from 1962-1990, the Staff performed two clear functions. First, it supported the DNRO with background, analysis, decision support, and technical advice. Second, it assisted the program offices in gathering information, working with the user community in defining and documenting intelligence and operational requirements, brokering meetings with the Washington community, offering suggestions, and facilitating meetings with NRO leadership.

Specifically relating to this delicate decision support role, Col Aubry McAlpine, the Deputy Director for Systems and Technology in the mid-1980s, offered his view as a consensus that was generally echoed by others who had collectively served across the history of the Staff:

> Jimmie Hill made it very clear that whatever came up from the program offices, our job was not to question it. He welcomed any explanation we could add. The staff was the staff, and we were not in that privileged chain between the Director, Mr. Hill, and the Program Directors. Although we did have expert technologists on the Staff…. John Capone, Jim Kindle, etc. The role they were used in though, especially by Jimmie, was to explain and elaborate but not confront the programs. We were not to quarrel with their positions or question them. This included the technical approach, as well as the financial approach. The Staff was therefore highly supportive of the program offices.[63]

On the other hand, nearly every DNRO sought to independently assess risks and choices among different program office options and to adjudicate between competing options. He often turned to the NRO Staff for analysis-based assistance and independent advice, but it was never sufficiently equipped to perform this function.

In examining the Staff's role in planning, studies, and analysis, one must differentiate between *community* studies, in which the Staff participated in broader efforts conducted by intelligence community elements, and *internal* NRO studies directed by the DNRO. In many cases, the NRO Staff members directly participated in community studies. In other instances, Staff participation focused on supporting and prepping the DNRO for his direct participation in community deliberations.

Even in the early years there were a number of NRO stakeholders who all advocated for their unique interests. Programs A, B, and C each had institutional interests in funding the evolution or improvement of the programs they were responsible for developing and operating. The user communities had interests. While the US Intelligence Board provided requirements, the NSA, DIA, and CIA were also strong independent champions for their needs.

63

Developing data to support planning decisions was difficult. Most of the data, along with the analytic models and decision aids, resided with the program offices and more specifically with the prime contractors developing each program. Thus, the DNRO often had to rely on the analytic capabilities nested initially within the contractors supporting the program offices.

Over the years there were different kinds of decisions that required studies and analysis. In many cases, the issue was relatively straightforward, such as the value of incremental upgrades to existing programs or the mission payload to put on the next passenger Sigint satellite. In some cases, the issue was whether or not and when to move to a new technology, such as from a film-based imagery system to an electro-optical solution. There were also choices among different phenomenology to address high-priority new missions, such as the response to a potential ABM deployment. In later years, analytic challenges often revolved around priorities for the allocation of scarce resources. This included decisions about support to military operations and whether and how missions might be combined to save costs — with consequences that could disproportionately impact or disadvantage the participation of the CIA, Air Force, or Navy elements of the NRO.

Although the designations and detailed responsibilities for plans, studies, and analysis changed over time,* there was always a lead planning organization on the Staff which drew from other Staff elements. In some cases, the Staff Director turned to an individual outside the primary planning organization, PEMs for example, to conduct a particular planning or study effort. Depending on its scope, program offices often provided representation, particularly when the effort required modeling and simulation support, since the Staff did not have any organic analytical capabilities.

The Early Years (1962-74). In 1963, shortly after the formation of the NRO and the NRO Staff, Brockway McMillan, in response to his frustration with what he perceived as the CIA's encroachment on NRO responsibilities, created the Advanced Planning Office within the Staff to "evaluate and recommend matters involving future space research and development projects."[64]

McMillan stressed that this Advanced Planning Office did not imply exclusive responsibility for such planning; however, this charter was a significant reach beyond what was to become the Staff's normal role in the decision process. According to historian Robert Perry, McMillan "thus tried to counterbalance attractive CIA Studies that might quickly be transformed into programs."[65] However, other than publishing the memorandum which created this Advanced Planning Office, there is no further accounting of this office within NRO historical records, and it was likely eliminated in 1965 when the NRO charter was re-written, McMillan departed, and the EXCOM was formed.

The late 1960s witnessed two major future planning decisions. The first involved high-altitude Sigint, and the second was the development of near real-time imagery. The Staff supported the DNROs development of recommendations and his participation in meetings, but the decisions were debated at the EXCOM and higher decision bodies.

The Film Read-out Gambit/Electro-Optical Imagery studies and debates are an example of the decision process at the time. Programs A and B presented their options, with competing analysis, different assessments of technical risk, and conflicting recommendations. The DNRO made a recommendation to the EXCOM which heard from both program offices. The decision was ultimately elevated to President Nixon, via the PFIAB and Henry Kissinger, for a decision in August 1971. Any deliberations by the Staff, or the DNRO for that matter, were overshadowed by the Land Committee and personal involvement by the CIA Director, the Secretary of Defense and his Deputy, and the

---

* Earlier examples of offices responsible for studies, plans, and analysis functions included Plans & Policy (1962-1963), Advanced Planning (1963-1974), Concepts and Applications (1974-1978), Research & Analysis (1978-1984), Long Range Plans (1984-1987), and Plans & Systems Development (1987-1989).

64

Secretary of State, as well as the White House Science Advisor, the Secretary of State, and the Director of OMB. The voice of the DNRO and his staff were lost in the cacophony of executive debate. Donald Regenhardt, an NRO Staff member at the time, recalled that the Staff's role was primarily that of an observer.[66] The decision ultimately favored the Program B recommendation for the EOI technology solution, which was the foundation for one of today's imaging systems.

> *"I don't know how the two of us could have been that wrong…*
> *but we were."*

It is interesting, in hindsight, that the Program A leadership came to agree with the decision. Maj Gen Ralph Jacobson (USAF, Ret.), the former Program A FROG Project Officer commented, "[Col] Lew Allen and I were running around trying to sell a program called FROG, which you may recall, and I don't know how the two of us could have been that wrong…but we were."[67]

In October 1970, NRO Director John L. McLucas created the Analysis Group.[68] This group, led by Dr. Robert Kahall, had an expanded role relative to the earlier Advanced Planning Office. In what can be surmised as a gesture to strengthen the group's authority, Director of the Analysis Group reported directly to the DNRO, instead of the Staff Director, supported by the assertion that the group would be responsible for studies and analyses of greater scope and duration than those of the NRO Staff. Unlike the previous Advanced Planning Office, McLucas' Analysis Group had a full complement of analysts in place with the arrival of the Analysis Group Director. In his memo to the group director, Dr. McLucas laid out an extremely ambitious list of tasks:

- Examine the product of our collection systems to determine whether satisfying the users' stated requirements is an adequate measure of our responsiveness to users' real needs… In making this determination it is important to differentiate between requirements stated as a result of technical possibilities and requirements expressing real needs.

- Determine whether we have or will have a proper mix of search, surveillance, high resolution, and immediate imagery recovery satellites to meet users' real needs….These questions can't be answered absolutely, but your group can assign costs per target and cost per square mile covered as some measure of effectiveness.

- Compare the roles of collection of imagery by satellite with collection by aircraft, manned and unmanned. Enumerate the proper roles of each type of vehicle and attempt to determine proper mixes.

- Attempt to establish better specifications for NRO vehicles by reviewing previous work and conducting analyses of the meanings, importance, and relevance of terms like contrast, ground resolution, ground sample distance, obliquity, and signal-to-noise in photographic imagery. These terms must be related to the users' functions like detection, recognition, and mensuration.[69]

Dr. John L. McLucas
DNRO: 17 Mar 1969 - 20 Dec 1973

The Analysis Group supported some EXCOM-sponsored studies, but there is no record of its having any effect on programmatic decisions. The organizational tug of war, primarily between the program offices' competing

65

performance/risk assessments and the lack of broadly accepted *analytically-based* studies and analyses, continued. The Analysis Group was disbanded in March 1974.

The Middle Years (1974–80). Following the dissolution of the Analysis Group, the new Staff Director, Brig Gen Jack Kulpa, established a Concepts and Applications Office within the NRO Staff. It was headed by widely respected Col Jim Blankenship and was composed of representatives from operational elements of each of the three services, as well as representatives of the intelligence community. It functioned primarily to assist "all elements of the NRO in developing a better understanding of the needs for and the uses of the products." Brig Gen Kulpa's motivation for creating the new office was to bring more focus on user needs, particularly those of the military services.[70]

The Concepts and Applications Office was an early leader in the demonstration of NRP support to military operations. It initiated a number of internally-led study and planning efforts with varying levels of community and NRO program office participation. It partnered with the military TENCAPs, and later the DSPO, in prioritizing and supporting defense-related initiatives.

One of the most notable NRO internal initiatives, conducted in the late 1970s, was the Multipurpose Mission Integrator study for the purpose of tasking resources. In that case, the Staff worked with the National Photographic Interpretation Center (NPIC) and COMIREX's Sigint Overhead Reconnaissance committee (SORS) to integrate near real-time Sigint external signals with photos to evaluate current and projected operational activities. Although the study was hindered by NSA's reluctance to provide weapons signals, it was an early precursor in demonstrating the utility of integrating signals and images as tipoff for targeting overhead resources. The Staff worked closely with Program A chief technologist, Bob Paulson, in integrating this Multipurpose Mission Integrator capability into the NRO Real-time Information Processor mobile vans, validating the operational value of real-time Sigint/Imint products to the military. This early demonstration of direct downlink of NRO data and of integrated products set the stage for optimizing the intelligence and operational value of NRO products and demonstrated that NRO systems could be operationally relevant. The Concepts and Applications office directly supported the newly formed NRO Tactical Exploitation of National Capabilities and Applications Program (NRO TENCAP), led by COL Ronald Lemanski (USA). This DSPO/TENCAP/NRO Staff partnership extended Brig Gen Kulpa's vision of making NRO national systems relevant to military operations.

During this period, the Staff also facilitated NRO support to a number of community studies aimed at defining architectural decisions. One example was the National Intelligence Plan for Satellites, in which the Staff coordinated and facilitated the NRO input for the IC Staff-led study.

Another example is the IC Staff-led Elint mix study which led the two-phased Elint study in 1979. The study was initiated to support decisions on the transition of all NRO satellites to a configuration compatible with the Space Shuttle. The first phase defined a composite set of Elint requirements, and the second sought to assess various options for future NRP Elint systems. An NRO Staff member, Air Force Captain Jim Beale, who was the PEM for the NRO's Elint satellites at the time, participated in all phases of the study and served as an interface between the program offices and the IC study lead. Program briefings and option requests were all arranged through the NRO Staff, and the staff lead reported progress directly to the DNRO. The study lasted through most of the year, and the results informed the FY 1980 President's Budget. The study offered several options, including a revolutionary low-orbit system that combined the missions of two legacy systems and an evolutionary option that involved existing systems. The DNRO included the evolutionary approach in his budget submission, but the DCI reversed his decision and included the revolutionary system in his final budget submission to the President. The SECDEF agreed with the DNRO and raised the issue to President Carter. To resolve this conflicting advice, the President asked his Science Advisor, Dr. Frank Press, to do an assessment and provide his recommendation. The NRO Staff lead was involved throughout the process, briefed the DNRO recommended approach to Dr. Press, and participated in deliberations leading to the final decision which endorsed the DNRO's recommended program.

66

The Later Years (1980–90). The Reagan-era goal of being able to fight and win a nuclear war generated many community studies. Topics ranged from missile defense and advanced technologies, to continuity of government and satellite survivability, to treaty verification. The Staff facilitated the NRO's participation and support for these community-led studies. One example was the survivability studies of the early 1980s, in response to National Security Decision Memorandum (NSDM) 333, Enhanced Survivability of Critical U.S. Military and Intelligence Space Systems. Lt Col Don Walker, in his initial assignment to the Staff,* assisted by Maj Mike Kemp, worked closely with other Staff elements, program offices, the IC Staff, and military elements in identifying and ranking various space and ground-segment initiatives for enhancing the survivability of NRO systems. In the end, however, although the NRO response was viewed as a thorough, objective response to the White House memorandum, Congress elected to continue funding NRO system performance initiatives, rather than investing in enhanced survivability.

Other examples of community-led efforts were the Arms Control studies and the related Strategic Relocatable Studies led by the Intelligence Community. According to Rick Buckley, the Deputy Director of Systems & Technology from 1986-89:

> Arms Control was another positive area of influence: [The] Staff provided good solid briefings of what we could and could not do. In [my] experience, this effort was the best coordinated government-wide decision-making process on intelligence support to policy of that era. It was one of the greatest contributions of the Staff, brokering honest communication that served as glue among very disparate problems and organizations.
>
> The Strategic Relocatable Target (SRT) Study was another study that related to the mobile missile study and effort. We worked with military elements on the ground. There was a good engineering analytic support capability that Program A provided. The Staff brought together various IC conversations, weeding out erroneous information, keeping the focus on facts that mattered.
>
> The lack of Staff analytic capabilities and a mature IC requirements integration/prioritization were limitations. There was a good partnership between Systems and Technology and the budget team. The major contribution was avoiding having our programs get influenced by Pentagon politics for budget resources. We were able to protect the programs.[71]

However, cooperation between the Staff and individual program offices began to rapidly erode during the early 1980s. This has been attributed to factors such as an influx of funds during the Reagan defense build-up, followed closely by the post-*Challenger* era in which discretionary funds were significantly reduced. Pete Aldridge, the DNRO during this period observed, "The program offices wouldn't take voluntary reductions. It was only the NRO Staff that had the independence to recommend an overall budget—they had to take more of a budgetary view of the whole NRO, as opposed to leaving those options up to the program offices, which they had been doing before. They kind of ran their own shops, and they had their own cost funding allocations…a period where they had more technology than money…creating a period of unhealthy competition."[72]

An example of an unsuccessful Staff-led study effort was the Future Sigint Capabilities Study (FSCS), directed by DNRO Aldridge in the mid-1980s. The objective of the FSCS was to define the future NRO

---

* It was not uncommon for Air Force officers to serve multiple assignments on the NRO Staff, first as field-grade staff officers, then later as NRO Staff Directors, as general officers. Examples are Major then Brig Gen Thomas Moorman, Lt Col then Maj Gen Donald Hard, and Lt Col then Brig Gen Donald Walker, the last three Staff Directors.

67

Sigint constellations in each of the three orbital regimes. The study went through three iterations with major participation by each of the three program offices. Predictably, the major issue surrounding each phase of the study was choice of the program office simulator to be used in evaluating each of the orbital alternatives. Finally, after much debate with little progress, DNRO Aldridge, frustrated with the lack of results, directed the Staff to arbitrate and provide a final report. The program office representatives refused to concur with the draft report, and FSCS died a natural death.[73]

Brig Gen Don Hard, the Staff Director under Pete Aldridge added, "while those battles were going on, the Staff was not in a position where we could adjudicate or even credibly comment on the relative merit of the various program proposals because we were at the mercy of the program offices, who had all the data, and their simulation results that proved their concept was better. Each program would come in and say "here's our data and here's our simulation, 'We're right; they're wrong.'"[74]

This competition, particularly between Program A and Program B, reached a new level of "unhealthiness" in the mid-1980s when Program B elected to challenge Program A, as well as the DNRO position for the upgrade to a Program A high-altitude Sigint program. The CIA challenge was only sustained after senior CIA managers took the issue directly to William Casey, the DCI, circumventing Pete Aldridge, the DNRO.

At this point, Aldridge, still influenced by the Air Force argument, and as some believe predisposed to maintaining parity between Programs A and B's share of NRO systems, directed the Staff to prepare a briefing for community decision leadership, including DCI Casey. According to Aubry McAlpine, Deputy Director for Systems and Technology:

> This was a program assigned to Program A, and Pete supported them. Mr. Aldridge knew he was going to have some issues with this and enlisted the Staff in a process to help validate his decision and to lay out his very orderly decision process. The issue was staffed in the IC, including NSA and also in DoD up to Casper Weinberger who then sent Maj Gen Colin Powell, his assistant, down to understand the issue. Gen Moorman, [McAlpine], and others were there in the meeting with Gen Powell. Weinberger signed off on Pete's decision. Julian Caballero had an alternative proposal. He expressed his concern about the way the Staff and Aldridge had made the decision. He [and Bob Kohler] went around Pete and went directly to Bill Casey. Mr. Casey got the decision thrown into a larger decision arena. The discussions ended up in the JCS Tank with the JCS, the SECDEF, and possibly the DCI. I briefed the program options. Mr. Aldridge was reversed on that decision, and the proposed architecture was built around Julian's proposal. Our job was to support the boss, rather than to conduct an independent assessment.[75]

This period of time, the mid- to late 1980s, was what DNRO Aldridge characterized as a period of "unhealthy competition that had developed between the program offices."[76] Many saw it as a period where the intelligence community began to outgrow the NRO's streamlined structure, including that of the NRO Staff, and one that began the call for a major restructuring of the NRO, including a more robust, independent studies and analysis capability. Martin Faga, who followed Pete Aldridge as DNRO in 1989, summarized, "The NRO Staff...operated as a *coordinating* office between independent programs. I had virtually no ability to analyze what program offices told me and had a very limited staff."[77]

Chapter 7

END OF THE BEGINNING: LAYING FOUNDATIONS FOR TODAY'S NRO

Some six weeks after becoming Director of the NRO in late September 1989, Martin Faga, witnessed the breaching of the Berlin Wall which cascaded to the demise of communism in Eastern Europe. On Christmas Day 1991, he witnessed the disbanding of the communist party in the USSR and the dissolution of the Soviet Union itself. Mr. Faga was responsible for guiding the NRO during this historic time and the aftermath of the collapse of the foes for which the NRO was largely formed. Mr. Faga graciously agreed to write the conclusion to this history of the NRO Staff. He made the early decisions that led to the reorganization of the NRO to better position it to meet the

Mr. Martin C. Faga, former DNRO

new realities and challenges of the post-Cold War era. The reorganization brought to a close the NRO Staff as it had existed for nearly thirty years—an elite staff that laid the solid foundation on which rests the staffing responsibilities carried out by successor NRO offices today.

I became Director of the National Reconnaissance Office in 1989 after 17 years of experience as a development engineer at NRO's Program B, a member of the NRO Staff, and service on the staff of the House Permanent Select Committee on Intelligence. With those long-term and close associations with the NRO, I arrived with a number of objectives that I hoped to accomplish. These included:

- Establishing a Plans and Analysis function in the NRO Staff to allow analysis in detail of proposals from the program offices to include technical, cost, and performance analysis. I moved early to do this, and I was rewarded with a high performing organization.

- Collocating the program offices. This had been recommended by the Geiger-Kelly Panel, commissioned by my predecessor, Pete Aldridge, and strongly pushed by the Congress. Like those recommending it, I thought this would improve coordination among the program offices and improve utilization of common technologies.

69

- Reducing or eliminating destructive competition between the program offices, particularly the Air Force and CIA offices, which I had witnessed during the previous 10 years.

- Continuing to provide strong support for the 10-year-old effort to improve Support to Military Operations, which had seen major investments by the services.

While these efforts were unfolding, the First Gulf War occurred, and space systems, including NRO systems, played a major role—all NRO systems were now near real-time and capable of supporting tactical operations. The war has been called by some writers as "the first space war," given that nearly all of the military and intelligence space capabilities were employed in tactical operations. This established tactical military forces as a demanding new "customer" for NRO data. While the ground war in Iraq ended in days, US military forces have been engaged in tactical operations in the region continuously since that time.

The experience of the war caused me to understand that the NRO could not properly serve the tactical customer as a "covert" organization. Moreover, at this point the "fact of" the NRO was still classified, but it was no secret. I came to view this "open secret" as corrosive to the many legitimate needs for security that existed within the NRO by making it difficult to distinguish between what was no longer sensitive and what truly remained sensitive. I sought to declassify the existence of the NRO, which was accomplished in September 1992.

In early 1992, the recently appointed Director of Central Intelligence, Robert Gates, asked Robert Fuhrman, then President of Lockheed, to lead a panel to examine the organization of the NRO. A major recommendation of the Panel was to organize the NRO around the intelligence disciplines. This would mean the end of structuring the NRO programs around the Air Force, CIA, and Navy elements. I had come to a similar conclusion based on observing how the systems began to overlap, and how the technologies available for new systems had become numerous. Clearly, we needed an overall architecture for national reconnaissance, which was nearly impossible to produce with the existing organization.

These tectonic changes in the NRO and its environment meant that the NRO Staff as we had known it—a very small group measured in the few dozens—would not be able to cope. We now had a vastly larger stakeholder group, new technological opportunities, expanded oversight within the Executive and by Congress, and a major reorganization.

The establishment of the NRO "INT-based" organization began in mid-1992 and extended beyond my departure in 1993. During this transition, the NRO Staff was absorbed into the appropriate functions of the new structure. The NRO has all of the functions that the earlier Staff provided, in some cases supplied or led by the same people. Nonetheless, the NRO Staff, about which we have written in this monograph, formally came to a close in 1992 when the last Director of the NRO Staff, Brig Gen Don Walker, departed.

The NRO Staff was ideal for the challenges of its time—the need to respond to a national security threat by developing a high priority program with demanding technology and short timelines. The Staff that emerged to deal with the threat was a small team with capable people who were empowered and worked within a highly classified environment. In the Staff existed the capacity to understand and explain programs, develop their budget and defend it throughout the government, develop supportive policy, and help conduct a robust security program.

70

Are there lessons to be learned from the 30-year experience with this kind of NRO Staff? Yes. This model has been used elsewhere, for example, by programs such as Naval Nuclear Propulsion and stealth aircraft programs, and could be used for future programs with similar challenges and circumstances.

With the dramatic world events and significant changes beginning in the 1990s, the "new" NRO looks quite different from its earlier form, requiring enhanced, distributed staff. It is much larger, integrated, and subject to the demands of a very large range of stakeholders. The NRO continues to enjoy strong support from the President and senior national security officials, a well-defined mission, a skilled government and contractor workforce and, most importantly, continued program success.[78]

71

Appendix 1

NRO STAFF DIRECTORS

1962-1978

Brig Gen John L. Martin, Jr., USAF
14 June 1962 — 2 August 1964

Brig Gen James T. Stewart, USAF
3 August 1964 – 1 February 1967

Brig Gen Russell A. Berg, USAF
1 February 1967 – 19 June 1969

Brig Gen Lew Allen. Jr., USAF
20 June 1969 – 20 August 1970

Col Edwin F. Sweeney, USAF
21 August 1970 – 31 May 1971

Brig Gen David D. Bradburn, USAF
1 June 1971 – 7 January 1973

Brig Gen John E. Kulpa, Jr., USAF
8 January 1973 – 30 September 1974

Col Harold P. Wheeler, USAF*
1 October 1974 – 18 March 1976

Brig Gen William L. Shields, Jr., USAF
18 March 1976 – 12 June 1978

*Colonel Robert Rosenberg was acting Director intermittently from 1 April 1975 to 1 March 1976 during Colonel Wheeler's frequent medical absences.

72

NRO STAFF DIRECTORS

1978-1992

Mr. Jimmie D. Hill

12 June 1978 – 9 April 1982

Brig Gen Donald D. Cromer, USAF

5 May 1982 – 11 June 1984

Col Paul F. Foley, USAF

15 June 1984 – 31 January 1985

Brig Gen Thomas. S. Moorman, Jr., USAF

5 February 1985 – 18 October 1987

Brig Gen Donald G. Hard, USAF

5 November 1987 – 5 February 1989

Brig Gen Donald R. Walker, USAF**

6 February 1989 – 1 Jan 1992

**Responsibilities of the NRO Staff began a physical and organizational transition in early 1990, culminating in a restructured NRO organization in 1992.

73

Appendix 2

OFFICE OF MISSILE AND SATELLITE SYSTEMS

The Office of Missile and Satellite Systems of the Secretary of the Air Force was the precursor of the NRO Staff, established approximately one year before formalization of the NRO, two years before the NRO Staff. It had primary responsibility for assisting the Air Force Secretary in discharging his responsibility for the direction, supervision, and control of the SAMOS Project. The Director of OMSS was responsible for maintaining liaison with the Office of the Secretary of Defense and other involved governmental agencies. Brigadier General Richard D. Curtin was the Director of this organization, located in the Pentagon.

Seated left to right: Col Charles Ruzeck, US Army; Col John L. Martin, USAF; Staff Director Brig Gen Richard D. Curtin, USAF: CAPT Frank B Gorman, US Navy.

Standing left to right: Lt Col Jack Sides, USAF; Lt Col Thomas J. Herron, USAF; Maj Clifton E. James, USAF; Capt Francis L. Lisciotti, USAF; Lt Col Edwin J. Istvan, USAF; Lt Col Charles H. Sinex, USAF; Lt Col Robert A. Van Mater, USAF; Maj Henry C. Howard, USAF

75

Although this photo has often been captioned as "The First Headquarters NRO Staff, Late 1961" it is actually General Curtin's Office of Missile and Satellite Systems, which later became the nucleus of the first NRO Staff, after the NRO Staff and NRO program offices were formerly created in September 1962.

Two abbreviations were used interchangeably for this same office: OMSS (Office of Missile and Satellite Systems) located in the Office of the Secretary of the Air Force, and also SAFMS (Secretary of the Air Force Missiles and Satellites). The following diagram depicts the organization of that early OMSS staff.

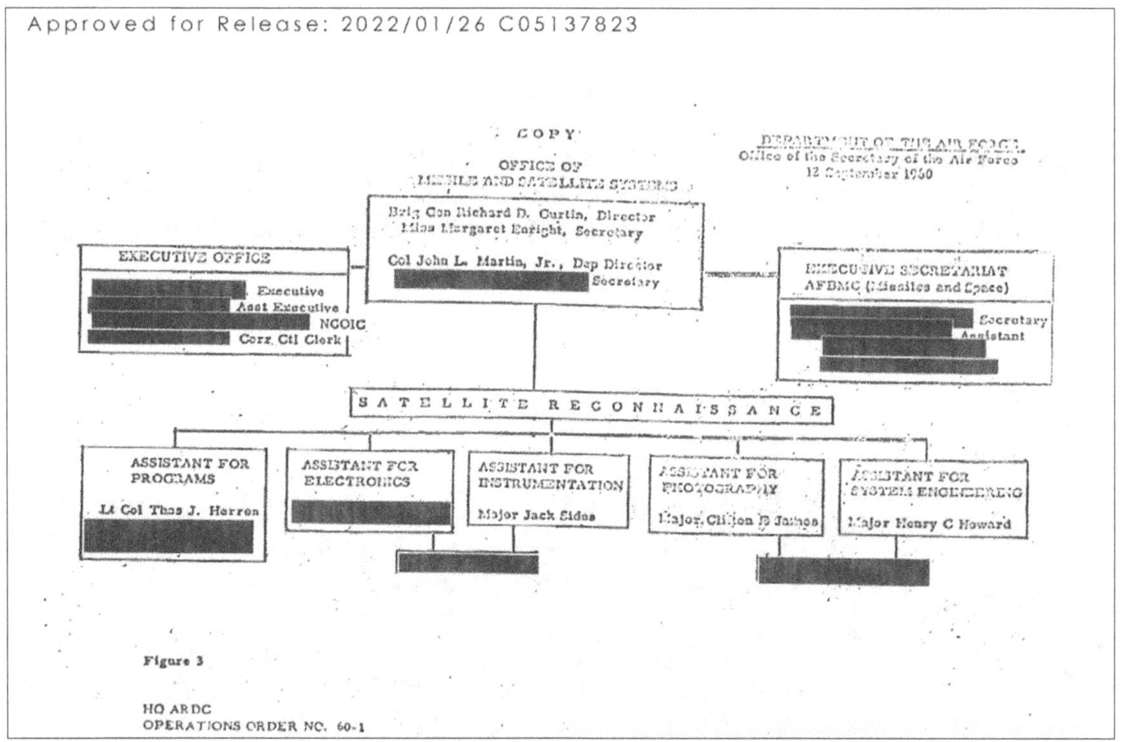

The responsibilities of the officers in that initial SAFMS/OMSS staff included:

- **Director** (Brig Gen Richard D. Curtin): Responsible for conducting all actions of SAFMS in accordance with policy and delegated authority from the Secretary.

- **Deputy Director** (Col John L. Martin, Jr.): Principal assistant to the Director acts with full authority of the Director on all affairs of SAFMS. Responsible for overall direction, guidance, supervision, and coordination of the activities of the office.

- **Executive**: Executive Officer and Chief of the Executive Office and responsible for the general administration of SAFMS, including mail, security, records, inspections, personnel, travel, and overall office management.

- **Asst. for Programs** (Lt Col Thomas J. Herron): Responsible for SAFMS duties concerning programming, funding, and schedules. Monitors, briefs and reports on all SAMOS launches. Maintains an active working SAMOS control room for daily use. Responsible for actions incident to revisiting, processing, and maintaining the SAMOS development plan. Responsible for general briefs on the entire overall SAMOS Project, and for the preparation and maintenance of complete briefing material, aids and information on the overall project.

- **Asst. for Electronics**: Responsible for SAFMS duties concerning electronic payloads, Elint, and related matters; weather aspects of the SAMOS Project; technical compatibility of the electronic aspects of Subsystem I, Space Ground Communications. Responsible for NSA liaison and coordination. Responsible for maintaining current knowledge of booster and vehicle capabilities. Alternate to the Assistant for Instrumentation.

- **Asst. for Photography**: (Maj Clifton E. James): Responsible for the SAMOS optical payload design and performance.

- **Asst. for Instrumentation** (Maj Jack Sides): Responsible for SAFMS duties concerning Subsystem I, its overall development, schedules, locations, tests, and overall technical design, overall data processing and handling of all SAMOS outputs. Also responsible for SAMOS recovery program, SAMOS command and control aspects, including centers and stations. Also responsible for MIDAS and Discoverer coordination. Alternative to Assistant for Electronics.

- **Asst. for System Engineering** (Maj Henry C. Howard): Responsible for overall system engineering aspects including interchangeability of payloads, system performance capabilities, mission variations, system growth possibilities, and relative priorities within the Project. Responsible for necessary coordination with related and supporting R&D programs. Also responsible for special projects as assigned by the Director. Alternative to the Assistant for Photography.

Reviewing the preceding position descriptions would lead one to believe that the Office of Missile and Satellite Systems, located within the Office of the Secretary of the Air Force was more of a line, rather than a staff organization, yet on the same day that OMSS was established, Secretary of the Air Force Order No. 115.1, 31 August 1960, designated Brig Gen Robert E. Greer as Director of the SAMOS Project, with duty station at Air Force Ballistic Missile Division in Los Angeles, as a field extension of the Office of the Secretary of the Air Force. The order specified that the Director of the SAMOS Project reported directly to the Secretary of the Air Force.

The total size of the original (pre-NRO) staff was 44 people, which included secretaries and airmen. It also included five individuals in Aircraft Projects and 14 in Operations, two functions that initially transferred to the NRO, but were eliminated in the mid-1970s.

Although the OMSS organization had different reporting channels, it was part of the organizational evolution that led to the National Reconnaissance Office and the NRO Staff. Several, but not all of the OMSS staff transitioned to the NRO Staff that was formally established on 23 July 1962.

77

Appendix 3

LIST OF INTERVIEWS

LAST NAME	FIRST NAME	NICKNAME	RETIRED RANK	INTERVIEW DATE
Aldridge	Edward C.	Pete	Civ	24 September 2013
Bailey	John	Jack	Col, USAF	9 July 2013
Barnett	James	Jim	CAPT, USN	27 June 2013
Beale	James	Jim	Brig Gen, USAF	10 January 2013
Berganini	David	Dave	Col, USAF	4 November 2013
Betterton	Thomas	Tom	RADM, USN	9 October 2013
Blankenship	James	Jim	Col, USAF	5 July 2013
Boehmer	Charles	Chuck	CAPT, USN	9 July 2013
Bracher	Phillip	Phil	Col, USAF	1 April 2014
Bryson	Jon		Col, USAF	5 November 2013
Buckley	Richard	Rick	Civ	17 October 2013
Charyk	Joseph		Civ	26 September 2014
Coglitore	Sebastian	Seb	Brig Gen, USAF	26 February 2014
Collier	Arthur	Art	CAPT, USN	3 December 2013
Conroy	Thomas	Tom	Civ	23 October 2013
Cromer	Donald	Don	Lt Gen, USAF	13 September 2013
Dahlen	Gary		Col, USAF	17 September 2013
Davis	Arthur	Art	Col, USAF	23 September 2013
Delpino	Joseph	Joe	CDR, USN	9 July 2013
Dionne	Gene		Col, USAF	17 September 2013
Donahue	Arnold	Arnie	Civ	4 November 2013
Eash	Joseph	Joe	Col, USAF	5 November 2013
Faga	Martin	Marty	Civ	20 June 2014
Fennell	Edward	Ed	Civ	29 October 2013
Fitzgibbon	James	Jim	Col, USAF	11 November 2014
Foley	Paul		Col, USAF	6 March 2014
Geiger	Robert	Bob	Lt Col, USAF	23 September 2013
Gilles	Gregory	Greg	Col, USAF	17 September 2013
Gordon	Harold	Hal	Col, USAF	7 March 2014
Gyauch	Charles	Chuck	Col, USAF	11 December 2013
Haas	Donald	Don	Civ	23 July 2013

LAST NAME	FIRST NAME	NICKNAME	RETIRED RANK	INTERVIEW DATE
Haas		Rich	Lt Col, USAF	10 July 2013
Hall	Keith		Civ	5 August 2013
Hard	Donald	Don	Maj Gen, USAF	23 September 2014
Hermann	Robert	Bob	Civ	22 May 2014
Hineman	Richard	Evans	Civ	20 June 2014
Hodgson	William	Mark	Col, USAF	17 September 2013
Hoskins	James	Jim	Capt, USAF	10 October 2013
Hutchison	Daniel	Dan	Col, USAF	3 March 2014
Jacobson	Ralph	Jake	Maj Gen, USAF	21 October 2013
Kohler	Robert	Bob	Civ	23 September 2013
Kulpa	John	Jack	Maj Gen, USAF	8 September 2013
Larned	Robert	Rick	Brig Gen, USAF	29 July 2013
Lopez	Lelio	Del	CAPT, USN	25 November 2013
McAlpine	Aubry		Col, USAF	4 February 2014
McMillan	Brockway		Civ	11 September 2014
Mericsko	Robert	Bob	Civ	3 February 2014
Moorman	Thomas	Tom	Gen, USAF	26 September 2013
Pattishall	Robert	Bob	Civ	29 September 2013
Paulson	Robert	Bob	Col, USAF	3 March 2014
Prochko	Robert	Bob	Lt Col, USAF	25 March 2014
Raspet	David	Dave	Col, USAF	12 September 2013
Regenhardt	John	Don	Col, USAF	7 February 2017
Riccardi	Fredrick	Fred	Col, USAF	23 September 2013
Rosenberg	Robert	Bob	Maj Gen, USAF	26 September 2013
Sharrard	John		Civ	6 February 2014
Skinner		Rick	Col, USAF	24 April 2014
Spence	Michael	Mike	Col, USAF	11 July 2013
Taylor	Richard	Rich	Civ	7 March 2014
Walker	Donald	Don	Brig Gen, USAF	26 September 2013
Watts	Sherilyn		Civ	5 March 2014
Wilhelm	Peter	Pete	Civ	15 November 2013

Appendix 4

NATIONAL INTELLIGENCE MERITORIOUS UNIT CITATION

National Intelligence Meritorious Unit Citation awarded to NRO Staff 1 August 2001 for its "collective superior performance for almost 35 years."

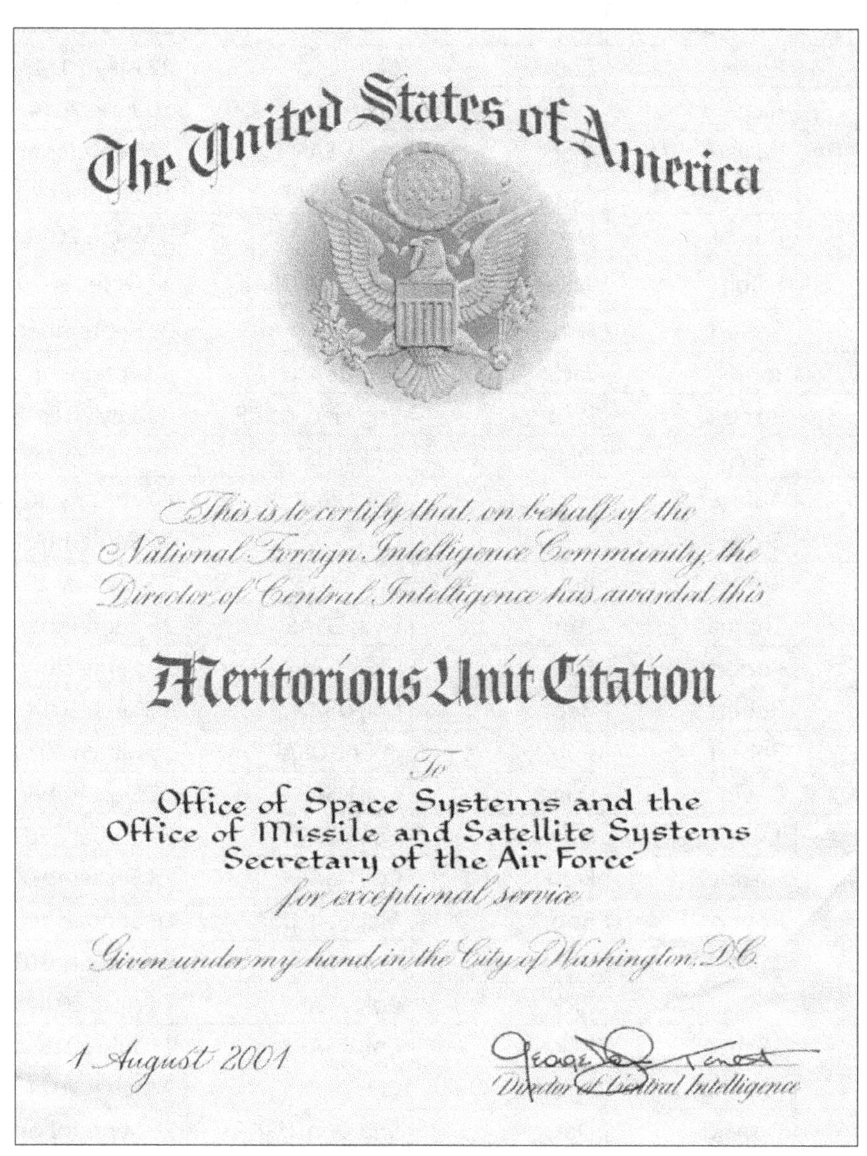

The United States of America
National Foreign Intelligence Community
Citation
OFFICE OF SPACE SYSTEMS AND THE
OFFICE OF MISSILE AND SATELLITE SYSTEMS
SECRETARY OF THE AIR FORCE
is hereby awarded the
NATIONAL INTELLIGENCE
MERITORIOUS UNIT CITATION
in recognition of its collective superior performance for almost thirty-five years, a period during which the United States has enjoyed superior technical advantage with space reconnaissance. The enduring quality of intelligence collection from space provided strategic and tactical policymakers and deployed military forces with a unique advantage over adversaries during the Cold War, through Desert Storm, and in all current military contingencies worldwide. The dedication and foresight of the Office guided the development and deployment of significant intelligence capabilities while pushing the envelope in advancing state-of-the-art technology and methods. It formulated the budgets for the programs and championed their approval in both Congress and the Executive Branch and established national policy and devised a strong security strategy for protection of sensitive and fragile collection activities. It conducted pioneering analysis and evaluation that crafted today's operational constellation of intelligence collection satellites and ground stations. Its contribution to this nation's defense is immeasurable and the legacy of what the Office of Space Systems and the Office of Missile and Satellite Systems accomplished remains a positive mark in national security, reflecting credit upon its members, the Central Intelligence Agency, the Department of Defense, and the Intelligence Community.

81

Appendix 5

CONTRIBUTORS

Principal Writers & Content Contributors

Col Robert Andrews, USAF (Ret.)

Brig Gen James R. Beale, USAF (Ret.)

Col Charles (Phil) Datema, USAF (Ret.)

The Honorable Mr. Martin C. Faga

Maj Gen Donald G. Hard, USAF (Ret.)

Gen Thomas S. Moorman, USAF (Ret.)

Contributing Writers

Maj Gen Phillip Bracher, USAF (Ret.)

Lt Gen Donald L. Cromer, USAF (Ret.)

Col Gary Dahlen, USAF (Ret.)

Brig Gen Robert E. (Rick) Larned, USAF (Ret.)

Col Fred Riccardi, USAF (Ret.)

Col Rick Skinner, USAF (Ret.)

Senior Review Panel

RADM Thomas C. Betterton, USN (Ret.)

Mr. R. Evans Hineman

Gen Thomas S. Moorman, Jr., USAF (Ret.)

Maj Gen Robert A. Rosenberg, USAF (Ret.)

Ms. Joanne O. Isham

Col Bill Savage, USAF (Ret.)

The Honorable Mr. Martin C. Faga

Col Donald Regenhardt, USAF (Ret.)

Brig Gen Donald Walker, USAF (Ret.)

Design & Layout and Editorial Support

Mr. Chuck Glover

Mr. Michael Suk

Security Consultant

Col Bob Andrews, USAF (Ret.)

Interviewers and Researchers

Brig Gen Jim Beale, USAF (Ret.)

Col Phil Datema, USAF (Ret.)

Ms. Joanne O. Isham

Col Bill Savage, USAF (Ret.)

83

Appendix 6

GLOSSARY

4C-1000	Pentagon: 4th Floor, Corridor C, Room 1000
ABM	Anti-Ballistic Missile
ACDA	Arms Control Disarmament Agency
ARPA	Advanced Research Projects Agency
ASAT	Anti-Satellite
ASPO	Army Space Program Office
BMD	Ballistic Missile Defense
BMDO	Ballistic Missile Defense Office
BYEMAN	Security codeword for compartmented NRO system information
CBJB	Congressional Budget Justification Book
CELV	Commercial (later, Complimentary) Expendable Launch Vehicle
CIA	Central Intelligence Agency
COMINT	Communications Intelligence
COMIREX	Committee for Imagery Requirements and Exploitation of USIB
CONUS	Continental United States
CSNR	Center for the Study of National Reconnaissance
DARPA	Defense Advanced Research Projects Agency
DCI	Director of Central Intelligence
DDNRO	Deputy Director of the NRO
DDS	Defense Dissemination System
DIA	Defense Intelligence Agency
DMA	Defense Mapping Agency
DNRO	Director of the NRO
DoD	Department of Defense
DRSP	Defense Reconnaissance Support Program
DSCS	Defense Satellite Communications System
DSPO	Defense Support Program Office
Elint	Electronic Intelligence (primarily Radar signals)

85

ELV	Expendable Launch Vehicle
EOI	Electro Optical Imagery
EXCOM	NRO Oversight Committee from 1965 -1974
FISINT	Foreign Instrumentation Signals Intelligence (e.g., telemetry)
FROG	Film Readout Gambit
FSCS	Future Sigint Capabilities Study
HPSCI	House Permanent Select Committee on Intelligence
ICBM	Intercontinental Ballistic Missile
ICRS	Imagery Collection Requirements sub-committee of the COMIREX
IC	Intelligence Community
IC Staff	The DCI's Staff supporting him in his community management role
Imint	Imagery Intelligence
IMINT	NRO Imagery Intelligence Systems Acquisition and Operations Directorate
IUS	Inertial Upper Stage
JCS	Joint Chiefs of Staff
KH	Keyhole (used as designator for different generations of imagery satellites)
NASA	National Aeronautics and Space Administration
NCP	National Cryptologic Program
NIP	National Intelligence Program (intelligence budget managed by DCI)
NPIC	National Photographic Interpretation Center
NRO	National Reconnaissance Office
NRO Staff	Secretary of the Air Force Space Systems (SAFSS)
NRP	National Reconnaissance Program (NRO budget)
NSA	National Security Agency
NSC	National Security Council
NSDM	National Security Decision Memorandum
OCMC	Overhead Collection Management Center
OD&E	CIA Office of Development and Engineering
OMB	Office of Management and Budget
OSD	Office of the Secretary of Defense
PCCB	Photo Configuration Control Board
PEM	Program Element Monitor
PFIAB	President's Foreign Intelligence Advisory Board
Program A	Secretary of the Air Force Special Projects (SAFSP)

Program B	CIA Office of Development and Engineering (OD&E)
Program C	Navy Space Project, Naval Electronics Systems Command
Program D	Joint CIA/USAF Aircraft overflight program
R&D	Research & Development
SAC	Strategic Air Command
SAF	Secretary of the Air Force
SAFSP	Secretary of the Air Force Special Projects
SALT	Strategic Arms Limitation Talks
SCI	Sensitive Compartmented Information
SDIO	Strategic Defense Initiative Organization
SECAF	Secretary of the Air Force
SECDEF	Secretary of Defense
SI	Signals Intelligence
Sigint	Signals Intelligence composed of Elint, Comint, and Fisint
SIGINT	NRO Signals Intelligence Systems Acquisition and Operations Directorate
SIGINT Committee	Committee of the USIB dealing with Signals Intelligence
SIOP	Single Integrated Operational Plan
SLV	Space Launch Vehicle
SOC	Satellite Operations Center
SOCOM	Special Operations Communications network
SORS	SIGINT Overhead Reconnaissance Committee of the SIGINT Committee
SPO	System Program Office
SRBM	Short Range Ballistic Missile
SSCI	Senate Select Committee on Intelligence
STS	Space Transportation System (Space Shuttle)
TCP	Technological Capabilities Panel
TENCAP	Tactical Exploitation of National Capabilities
TK	Talent-Keyhole (Compartment for NRO-derived product information)
USAF	United States Air Force
USD	Under Secretary of Defense
USECAF	Under Secretary of the Air Force
USIB	United States Intelligence Board
USSR	Union of Soviet Socialist Republics
WS-117L	Weapon System 117L

ENDNOTES

1   Faga, Martin, Prepared paper for the DNI, "National Reconnaissance Views," June 2009.

2   Ibid.

3   Eisenhower, Dwight D., Memorandum for the Secretary of State, The Secretary of Defense, The Attorney General, the Chairman, Atomic Energy Commission, and the Director of Central Intelligence, 26 August 1960.

4   Wheeler, Harold P., Point paper for DNRO James Plummer, 20 January 1976.

5   Faga, Martin, phone interview by Phil Datema, 18 September 2020.

6   Gilpatric, Roswell L. and Dulles, Allen W., Memorandum, "Management of the National Reconnaissance Program," 6 September 1961.

7   Charyk, Joseph V., Memorandum, "Organizations and Functions of the NRO," 23 July 1962.

8   Faga, June 2009.

9   Charyk, Joseph V., Interview by Datema, Isham, and Beale, 26 September 2014.

10   Perry, Robert L., *A History of Satellite Reconnaissance*, 2012, p 146.

11   Charyk, 26 September 2014.

12   Ibid.

13   Buckley, Richard, Interview by Datema and Isham, 17 October 2013.

14   Ibid.

15   Faga, Martin, Statement at monograph senior review, 20 June 2014.

16   Dahlen, Gary, Interview of Gary Dahlen, Mark Hodgson, Gene Dionne, Greg Gilles by Phil Datema, 17 September 2013.

17   Perry, 2012, p 53.

18   Moorman, Thomas, Interview by Phil Datema, 17 January 2019.

19   Laurie, Clayton D., *Congress & the National Reconnaissance Office*, June 2001.

20   Berkowitz, Bruce, *The National Reconnaissance Office at 50 Years, A Brief History*, July 2018, pp 13-14.

21   Regenhardt, John D., Interview by Datema and Savage, 7 February 2017.

22   Faga, Martin, Interview by Patrick Widlake, 6 May 2006.

23   Laurie, 2001, p 1.

24   Ford, Gerald R., Executive Order 11905, "United States Foreign Intelligence Activities," 18 February 1976.

25   Faga, 6 May 2006.

26   Charyk, 26 September 2014.

27   McMillan, Brockway, Memorandum, "Memorandum to Director, NRO Staff, Advanced Planning for the NRP," 10 December 1963.

89

28   Perry, Robert L., *Management of the National Reconnaissance Program 1960-1965*, Chapter Five, Years of Acrimony, 11 September 2018, p 76.

29   Kulpa, John E., Memorandum, "Organizational and Functional Changes to the NRO Staff," 6 March 1974.

30   Mark, Hans, Memorandum, "NRO Staff Reorganization," 14 April 1978.

31   Mark, Hans, Memorandum, "Functional Reorganization of the NRO Staff," 30 May 1978.

32   Charyk, 23 July 1962.

33   Ibid.

34   Walker, Donald R., Interview by Datema et. al., 26 September 2013.

35   McCone, John A. and Gilpatric, Roswell L., "Agreement Between Secretary of Defense and the Director of Central Intelligence on Responsibilities of the National Reconnaissance Office," 2 May 1962.

36   Swan, Cathy W. and Swan Peter A., *Birth of Air Force Satellite Reconnaissance: Facts, Recollections and Reflections*, Summer 2015, p. 57; and Cohen, Harvey, Interviews by Phil Datema, early 2017.

37   Riccardi, Fred, Telephone interview by Phil Datema, 2013.

38   Hard, Donald G., Email to Phil Datema, 21 September 2020.

39   Bracher, Phil, Telephone interview by Phil Datema, September 2020.

40   Moorman, Thomas S., Interview by Phil Datema, 17 January 2019.

41   Perry, 2012, p 42.

42   Ibid, p 70.

43   Worthman, Paul, Memorandum for Record, "SAFSL (MOL Program/SAFSS (NRO Staff) Relationships," 9 July 1965.

44   Moorman, Thomas S., Interview by Donald Hard, 16 May 2019.

45   Aldridge, Edward C., Interview by Donald Hard, 16 May 2019.

46   Fitzgibbon, James, Interview by Isham and Savage, 11 March 2015.

47   Walker, Donald R., Email to Phil Datema, 2 March 2014.

48   Perry, 2018.

49   Charyk, 26 September 2014.

50   Gyauch, Chuck, Interview by Datema, Savage, and Isham, 11 December 2013.

51   Hall, Keith R., Interview by Datema and Isham, 5 August 2013.

52   Martin, John L., Memorandum for NRO Staff, Subject: "Responsibilities of the NRO Communications Staff Officer and NRO Executive Officer," 27 May 1964.

53   Opfer, James, Interview by Phil Datema, 7 September 2020.

54   Martin, John L., 27 May 1964.

55   Bradburn, David D., Memorandum, "Description of Duties – NRO Communications Officer," Undated, circa 1971.

56   Regenhardt, John D., Interview with Datema and Savage, 7 February 2014 and 4 October 2018.

57   Dahlen, Gary, Email to Phil Datema, 1 November 2015.

58   Ibid.

59   Anderson, David, Telephone and email interviews by Phil Datema, 2020.

60   Pattishall, 27 September 2013.

61   Hoskins, James, Interview by Datema and Isham, 10 October 2013.

62   Ibid.

63   McAlpine, Aubry, Interview with Datema and Isham, 4 February 2014.

64   McMillan, 10 December 1963.

65   Perry, 11 September 2018, p 76.

66   Regenhardt, John D., Interview with Phil Datema, 20 June 2014.

67   Jacobson, Ralph H., Interview with Phil Datema, 21 October 2013.

68   McLucas, John L., Memorandum, "Analysis Group Projects," 30 October 1970.

69   Ibid.

70   Kulpa, 6 March 1974.

71   Buckley, 17 October 2013.

72   Aldridge, Edward C., Interview by Datema, Isham, and Savage, 24 September 2013.

73   Killoran, Lance, Telephone interview by Phil Datema, 7 October 2003.

74   Hard, Donald G., Interview by Phil Datema, 23 September 2014.

75   McAlpine, 4 February 2014.

76   Aldridge, 24 September 2013.

77   Faga, 6 May 2006.

78   Martin C. Faga, Director, National Reconnaissance Office, 28 September 1989 – 5 March 1993.

INDEX

93

94

G

H

I

J

K

L

95

M

N

O